TO
DAVID ARCHER

CONTENTS

ACKNOWLEDGEMENTS 13

INTRODUCTION 15

SELECTED BIOGRAPHICAL NOTES 19

I

W. H. AUDEN

In Memory of W. B. Yeats 23
Gonzalo (*From* The Sea and the Mirror) 25
Song for St Cecilia's Day 27
Ode to Gaea 30
The Shield of Achilles 33

JOHN BETJEMAN

Upper Lambourne 36
Bristol 36
Youth and Age on Beaulieu River, Hants 37
I. M. Walter Ramsden, Ob. March 26, 1947,
    Pembroke College, Oxford 38

NORMAN CAMERON

Forgive Me, Sire 40
Three Love Poems 40
The Firm of Happiness, Limited 41
Green, Green is El Aghir 42

ROY CAMPBELL

Luis de Camões 43
En Una Noche Oscura 43
November Nights 45

WILLIAM EMPSON

Autumn on Nan-Yueh 46

CONTENTS

ROBERT GRAVES

A Plea to Boys and Girls   54
Dialogue on the Headland   54
Beauty in Trouble   55
A Love Story   56
She Tells Her Love While Half Asleep   57
1805   57

HUGH MACDIARMID

From In Memoriam James Joyce
Let the only consistency   59
And, above all, Karl Kraus   62
The world is fast bound in the snares of Varuna   66

LOUIS MACNEICE

Brother Fire   70

EDWIN MUIR

The Annunciation   71
Orpheus' Dream   72
The Child Dying   72

WILLIAM PLOMER

Sounds of Pleasure: Cannes, 1938   74

STEVIE SMITH

Not Waving But Drowning   77
Away, Melancholy   77
My Heart Goes Out   79
Songe D'Athalie   79
Childe Rolandine   80
Thoughts about the Person from Porlock   81
In the Park   83

CONTENTS

VERNON WATKINS

Swedenborg's Skull	85
The Feather	86
Indolence	87
The Death Bell	87

2

GEORGE BARKER

The True Confession of George Barker	97

THOMAS BLACKBURN

A Small, Keen Wind	126
Teaching Wordsworth	126

MAURICE CARPENTER

To S.T.C. on his 179th Birthday, October 12, 1951	129

CHARLES CAUSLEY

On Seeing a Poet of the First World War on the Station at Abbeville	132

LAWRENCE DURRELL

On First Looking Into Loeb's Horace	133

ROY FULLER

What is Terrible	136

DAVID GASCOYNE

An Elegy	138
The Gravel-Pit Field	140
Ecce Homo	142
A Vagrant	144
The Sacred Hearth	146

CONTENTS

W. S. GRAHAM

The Ballad of Baldy Bane   148

JOHN HEATH-STUBBS

To My Brother in Rhodesia   154
Use of Personal Pronouns: A Lesson in
     English Grammar   154

PATRICK KAVANAGH

Intimate Parnassus   158
Shancoduff   159
On Looking into E. V. Rieu's Homer   159
Epic   160
Kerr's Ass   160
The Hero   161
Lines Written on a Seat on the Grand Canal,
     Dublin   163
The Hospital   163
Living in the Country   164

F. T. PRINCE

Soldiers Bathing   167

C. H. SISSON

Money   169
Sparrows Seen from an Office   169
Moriturus   170
What a Piece of Work is Man   170

DYLAN THOMAS

The Hunchback in the Park   173
Do not Go Gentle into that Good Night   174
Vision and Prayer   175

CONTENTS

3

DANNIE ABSE

Letter to Alex Comfort   185
The Game   186

DRUMMOND ALLISON

Verity   188
Dedication   188

J. C. ASHBY

Please Don't Laugh   189

WILLIAM BELL

Christmas Elegy   191

ANTHONY CRONIN

Lines for a Painter   193
Elegy for the Nightbound   194
Responsibilities   195

DONALD DAVIE

Barnsley & District   198

KEITH DOUGLAS

The Deceased   200

THOM GUNN

On the Move   201

MICHAEL HAMBURGER

Solidarity   203

BRIAN HIGGINS

The North   204

CONTENTS

GEOFFREY HILL

Genesis 210
Canticle for Good Friday 212
A Pastoral 212

TED HUGHES

Six Young Men 214
Hawk Roosting 215

ELIZABETH JENNINGS

Song at the Beginning of Autumn 217

SIDNEY KEYES

The Island City 218

PHILIP LARKIN

At Grass 219

CHRISTOPHER LOGUE

From Book XXI of Homer's *Iliad* 220

DOM MORAES

Two Christmas Sonnets:
Santa Claus 228
Family Dinner 228

MARTIN SEYMOUR-SMITH

Found on a Building Site 230
The Administrators 230
Request on the Field 232

CHARLES TOMLINSON

On the Hall at Stowey 233

ANTHONY THWAITE

The Plausible Bird 236

ACKNOWLEDGEMENTS

For permission to publish or reproduce the poems in this anthology acknowledgement is made to the following:

For W. H. Auden to Faber & Faber Ltd (*Another Tide, For the Time Being, Collected Shorter Poems*, and *Shield of Achilles*); for John Betjeman to John Murray (*Collected Poems*); for Norman Cameron to Chatto & Windus Ltd and the Hogarth Press (*Collected Poems*); for Roy Campbell to Faber & Faber Ltd (*Talking Bronco*), The Harvill Press and The Bodley Head Ltd (*Collected Poems of Roy Campbell, Volume Two*); for William Empson to Chatto & Windus Ltd (*Collected Poems*); for Robert Graves to Cassell & Co. Ltd (*Collected Poems 1959*); for Hugh MacDiarmid to the author; for Louis Macneice to Faber & Faber Ltd (*Collected Poems*); for Edwin Muir to Faber & Faber Ltd; for William Plomer to Jonathan Cape (*Collected Poems*); for Stevie Smith to André Deutsch Ltd, Longmans, Green & Co. Ltd (*Selected Poems*), and the author; for Vernon Watkins to Faber & Faber Ltd (*Death Bell, Lady and Unicorn, The Ballad of the Mari Llwyd*, and *Cypress and Acacia*); for George Barker to the author; for Thomas Blackburn to Putnam & Co. Ltd; for Maurice Carpenter to Elek Books Ltd; for Charles Causley to Rupert Hart-Davis Ltd (*Union Street*); for Lawrence Durrell to Faber & Faber Ltd (*Collected Poems*); for Roy Fuller to The Hogarth Press (*A Lost Season*); for David Gascoyne to the author; for W. S. Graham to Faber & Faber Ltd (*The Nightfishing*); for John Heath-Stubbs to the Oxford University Press (*The Blue Fly in His Head*) and Methuen & Co. Ltd (*A Charm Against The Toothache*); for Patrick Kavanagh to Longmans, Green & Co. Ltd (*Collected Poems*) and the author; for F. T. Prince to The Fortune Press; for C. H. Sisson to Abelard-Schuman Ltd (*The London Zoo*) and the author; for Dylan Thomas to J. M. Dent & Sons Ltd (*Collected Poems*); for Dannie Abse to Hutchinson & Co. Ltd (*Walking Under Water*); for Drummond Allison to The Fortune Press (*The Yellow Night*) and to C. R. Allison; for J. C. Ashby to the author; for William Bell to Faber & Faber Ltd (*Mountains Beneath the Horizon*); for Anthony Cronin to The Cresset Press (*Poems*) and to the author; for Donald Davie to the author; for Keith Douglas to the author's mother and Faber & Faber Ltd; for Thom Gunn to Faber & Faber Ltd (*Sense of Movement*); for Michael Hamburger to Longmans, Green & Co. Ltd (*Weather and Season*); for Brian Higgins to Abelard-Schuman Ltd (*The Only Need*); for Geoffrey Hill to André Deutsch Ltd (*The*

ACKNOWLEDGEMENTS

Unfallen); for Ted Hughes to Faber & Faber Ltd (*Lupercal* and *Hawk in the Rain*); for Elizabeth Jennings to André Deutsch Ltd (*A Way of Looking*); for Sidney Keyes to Routledge & Kegan Paul Ltd (*Collected Poems*); for Philip Larkin to The Marvell Press (*The Less Deceived*); for Christopher Logue to Hutchinson & Co. Ltd; for Dom Moraes to the author; for Martin Seymour-Smith to Abelard-Schuman Ltd (*Tea With Miss Stockport*); for Charles Tomlinson to the Oxford University Press (*Seeing is Believing*); and for Anthony Thwaite to The Marvell Press (*Home Truths*).

INTRODUCTION

ENGLISH poetry of the last twenty years is considerably more varied and alive than is generally realized or admitted. In spite of the myth about the difficulty of getting verse published, more of it was printed than in any other two decades of English literature. It is a commonplace that at any one time there are few genuine poets compared with the many who have talent; and one result of the large crop of published volumes of verse has been to make it difficult to see the trees for the wood. Some of those who have written the best poetry of the time under review have been overlooked or neglected either because they published little or because their work ran counter to the various literary fashions – and there were an extraordinary number of these – which succeeded one another in daft profusion during the war years and after. Cases in point are Patrick Kavanagh and Stevie Smith; while poets like Hugh MacDiarmid and George Barker, who made their names before 1940 but produced – certainly in the case of Barker – their best poetry after this date, have been curiously undervalued. I have not hesitated to allocate them rather more space than has been fashionable in recent anthologies, at the expense of cutting down or excluding better-known writers whose ambience, and best work, seems to belong to the thirties rather than the period covered by this anthology.

There is nothing to be gained by producing yet another anthology to cover familiar ground; indeed one function of an anthology is to draw attention to little-known or neglected poems of cardinal merit. The drawback of most anthologies is that they tend for obvious reasons to give preference to short 'anthology-sized' pieces, and as a result present a wrong impression of the poetry written in any given period. The long poem is a different medium from the lyric or short piece, and produces statements of a different kind. I have therefore included a fair number, preferring to represent, for example, Empson by his rumbustious *Autumn on Nan-Yueh* than by a selection of his shorter poems which are both well-known and adequately anthologized elsewhere; MacDiarmid by extracts from *In Memoriam James Joyce*, a poem that has not yet received its due and is not easily available; Barker by *The True Confession of George Barker*, which, though generally recognized as the most remarkable long poem of the mid-century, is not included in his *Collected Poems*. And if I had the room I should have liked to include Vernon Watkins's *The Ballad of the Mari Llwyd* and Patrick Kavanagh's *The Great Hunger*. The last two decades have indeed been prolific in long poems of merit. To take an obvious example, T. S. Eliot's *Four Quartets* definitely belongs to the period covered by this anthology, as do Ezra Pound's later *Cantos*. But I have, for self-evident reasons, excluded these founding fathers of modern poetry and limited my choice (with the exception of the late Edwin Muir, who began writing verse late in life and most of whose work appeared in the last twenty years) to poets born after 1890.*

In the last half-century two major historical events have created a profound difference in the spiritual conditioning of those who spent their childhood or reached adolescence before they took place. The first was the disruption of Europe, with the mores and values that attended it, in 1914–18; the second, the explosion of the atomic device in 1945. Those whose childhood was over by 1918, those who had grown up by 1940, and those whose infancy or adolescence coincided with the bomb, were conditioned by entirely different spiritual climates, as different as those which existed in Europe before and after the French Revolution. Roughly speaking it may be said that the first group still believes in Eden, the second expects apocalypse, while for the third, to judge from a certain stunned withdrawal that seems to characterize its poetry, apocalypse has already occurred. It was not to underline this phenomenon that I divided the poets in this anthology into three chronological groups (the first contains the work of poets born before 1910, the second those born before 1920, and the last poets born after that date). My original idea was to separate the three voices – age, maturity, and youth – to demonstrate the difference of the response of each to the two decades covered by the anthology. And it seemed to me that in selecting, without reference

* Any list of outstanding long poems of the mid-century should include *The Anathemata* by David Jones. Though I have to confess it is still one of my blind spots.

to the stylistic shibboleths of those analytic critics who devote their attention to secondary considerations – e.g. the structure rather than content of poems – those which seemed to me the best, there might emerge a report on the human condition, an indication of the imaginative response to the contemporary dilemma; and this not necessarily to be found only in those poems which refer directly to current events.

The artist, as Pound has said, is the antennae of the race. The reason why poetry is important is that it is the most efficient instrument of both discovery and expression that exists. But nobody has yet come up with a satisfactory definition of poetry. Even Pound gave it up: 'All criticism should be professedly personal criticism. In the end the critic can only say "I like it" or "I am moved" or something of that sort. . . . On closer analysis I find that I mean something like "maximum efficiency of expression"; I mean that the writer has expressed something interesting in such a way that one cannot re-say it more efficiently. I also mean something associated with discovery. The artist must have discovered something – either of life itself or the means of expression.' That last sentence is the formula by which the poems here collected have been chosen.

There are no American poets in this anthology. American and English poetry is no longer homogeneous, though written in approximately the same language. Contemporary American poetry – which, thanks to the excessive interest taken in it by American universities, is now an industry rather than an art – seems to be wandering off in the direction of the decorative, where style and technique is all and thought, if anything, a peg on which to hang a Chinese box of semantic ingenuities. It is not that the artist must not be craftsman, but that craftsmanship is not all.

Poetry is not entertainment but is meant for enjoyment. There are many reasons why people write poetry but only one good reason why they should read it. Enjoyment and entertainment are distinct affairs, and those conditioned only to the latter may never experience the former.

March, 1962   DAVID WRIGHT

SELECTED BIOGRAPHICAL NOTES

SOME of the poets in this anthology may be unfamiliar either because they are unduly neglected or have yet to make their names; while some died young. J. C. Ashby began writing poetry only a few years ago – rebarbative verse which is an uncomfortable exploration of provincial suburban life. His only published poems have appeared in the quarterly review *X*. 'I was born (physically) on 10.11.1919; my education was mainly at elementary schools and third-rate private schools. Is the fact that I was seventeen years a cowman of any interest?' he wrote when I asked for biographical information. Drummond Allison was born in 1923 and killed in 1943. His collection of poems, *The Yellow Night*, was published posthumously in the same year. He was a friend of Sidney Keyes (1922–43) who was also killed in the war. Keyes was the better known poet, but Allison may have been the greater loss. William Bell was born in 1924 and killed climbing the Matterhorn in 1948. Like Keyes and Allison he was educated at Oxford, though not at the same time. By coincidence he lodged at the same digs, 52 High Street, as they did; after his death the landlady refused to take any more undergraduate poets, being understandably upset by the rate of mortality. Bell's posthumous volume of poems, *Mountains Beneath the Horizon*, was published by Faber and edited by his friend John Heath-Stubbs. Maurice Carpenter was born in 1911. His first book, *IX Poems*, was printed on a hand-press by his friend George Barker. He has also published *The Tall Interpreter*, a fragment of an ambitious long poem; and *The Indifferent Horseman*, a study of Coleridge. Anthony Cronin was born in 1925 at Enniscorthy in Ireland. The Cresset Press published his *Poems* in 1958; a partly autobiographical novel, *The Life of Riley*, was published by Secker and Warburg in 1964. W. S. Graham was born in 1917 at Glasgow; his two most recent books of poems, *The White Threshold* and *The Night-fishing*, were published by Faber. 'Born at Batley in 1930, bored at Bradford in 1940, in 1950 he had an affair with the gamma function. He was educated in 1960 at the "York Minster", Soho,' states the biographical note on the endpaper of Brian Higgins's first book of poems, *The Only Need*. He died only

19

five years later of a rare condition of the heart just before the publication of *The Northern Fiddler* (Methuen), his third book of poems, which was made a posthumous choice of the Poetry Book Society. Martin Seymour-Smith was born in 1928 and educated at Oxford. For some years he was tutor to Robert Graves's children at Mallorca. His second book of poems, *Tea with Miss Stockport*, was published in 1963; he has also published an edition of Shakespeare's *Sonnets* in the original spelling. C. H. Sisson was born at Bristol in 1914, educated at elementary schools and Bristol University. He is at present Under-Secretary in the Ministry of Employment and Productivity. He has published three volumes of poems and a remarkable novel, *Christopher Homm* (Methuen), besides translations of Heine and Catullus and an authoritative work on government: *The Spirit of British Administration* (Faber). At present he is writing a history of English poetry in the twentieth century.

ONE

W. H. AUDEN

In Memory of W. B. Yeats
(d. January 1939)

I

He disappeared in the dead of winter:
The brooks were frozen, the airports almost deserted,
And snow disfigured the public statues;
The mercury sank in the mouth of the dying day.
O all the instruments agree
The day of his death was a dark cold day.

Far from his illness
The wolves ran on through the evergreen forests,
The peasant river was untempted by the fashionable quays;
By mourning tongues
The death of the poet was kept from his poems.

But for him it was his last afternoon as himself,
An afternoon of nurses and rumours;
The provinces of his body revolted,
The squares of his mind were empty,
Silence invaded the suburbs,
The current of his feeling failed: he became his admirers.

Now he is scattered among a hundred cities
And wholly given over to unfamiliar affections,
To find his happiness in another kind of wood
And be punished under a foreign code of conscience;
The words of a dead man
Are modified in the guts of the living.

But in the importance and noise of tomorrow
When the brokers are roaring like beasts on the floor of the Bourse,
And the poor have the sufferings to which they are fairly accustomed,

And each in the cell of himself is almost convinced of his freedom,
A few thousand will think of this day
As one thinks of a day when one did something slightly unusual.
O all the instruments agree
The day of his death was a dark cold day.

2

You were silly like us: your gift survived it all;
The parish of rich women, physical decay,
Yourself; mad Ireland hurt you into poetry.
Now Ireland has her madness and her weather still,
For poetry makes nothing happen; it survives
In the valley of its saying where executives
Would never want to tamper; it flows south
From ranches of isolation and the busy griefs,
Raw towns that we believe and die in; it survives,
A way of happening, a mouth.

3

Earth, receive an honoured guest;
William Yeats is laid to rest:
Let the Irish vessel lie
Emptied of its poetry.

Time that is intolerant
Of the brave and innocent,
And indifferent in a week
To a beautiful physique,

Worships language and forgives
Everyone by whom it lives;
Pardons cowardice, conceit,
Lays its honours at their feet.

Time that with this strange excuse
Pardoned Kipling and his views,
And will pardon Paul Claudel,
Pardons him for writing well.

In the nightmare of the dark
All the dogs of Europe bark,
And the living nations wait
Each sequestered in its hate;

Intellectual disgrace
Stares from every human face,
And the seas of pity lie
Locked and frozen in each eye.

Follow, poet, follow right
To the bottom of the night,
With your unconstraining voice
Still persuade us to rejoice;

With the farming of a verse
Make a vineyard of the curse,
Sing of human unsuccess
In a rapture of distress;

In the deserts of the heart
Let the healing fountain start,
In the prison of his days
Teach the free man how to praise.

From *The Sea and the Mirror*

GONZALO

Evening, grave, immense, and clear
Overlooks our ship whose wake
Lingers undistorted on

Sea and silence; I look back
For the last time as the sun
Sets behind that island where
All our loves were altered: yes,
My prediction came to pass,
Yet I am not justified,
And I weep but not with pride.
Not to me the credit for
Words I uttered long ago
Whose glad meaning I betrayed;
Truths today admitted, owe
Nothing to the councillor
In whose booming eloquence
Honesty became untrue.
Am I not Gonzalo who
By his self-reflection made
Consolation an offence?

There was nothing to explain:
Had I trusted the Absurd
And straightforward note by note
Sung exactly what I heard,
Such immediate delight
Would have taken there and then
Our common welkin by surprise,
All would have begun to dance
Jigs of self-deliverance.
It was I prevented this,
Jealous of my native ear,
Mine the art which made the song
Sound ridiculous and wrong,
I whose interference broke
The gallop into jog-trot prose
And by speculation froze
Vision into an idea,
Irony into a joke,

Till I stood convicted of
Doubt and insufficient love.

Farewell, dear island of our wreck.
All have been restored to health,
All have seen the Commonwealth,
There is nothing to forgive.
Since a storm's decision gave
His subjective passion back
To a meditative man,
Even reminiscence can
Comfort ambient troubles like
Some ruined tower by the sea
Whence boyhoods growing and afraid
Learn a formula they need
In solving their mortality,
Even rusting flesh can be
A simple locus now, a bell
The Already There can lay
Hands on if at any time
It should feel inclined to say
To the lonely – 'Here I am,'
To the anxious – 'All is well.'

Song for St Cecilia's Day

I

In a garden shady this holy lady
With reverent cadence and subtle psalm,
Like a black swan as death came on
Poured forth her song in perfect calm:
And by occan's margin this innocent virgin
Constructed an organ to enlarge her prayer,
And notes tremendous from her great engine
Thundered out on the Roman air.

Blonde Aphrodite rose up excited,
Moved to delight by the melody,
White as an orchid she rode quite naked
In an oyster shell on top of the sea;
At sounds so entrancing the angels dancing
Came out of their trance into time again,
And around the wicked in Hell's abysses
The huge flame flickered and eased their pain.

Blessed Cecilia, appear in visions
To all musicians, appear and inspire:
Translated Daughter, come down and startle
Composing mortals with immortal fire.

2

I cannot grow
I have no shadow
To run away from,
I only play.

I cannot err;
There is no creature
Whom I belong to,
Whom I could wrong.

I am defeat
When it knows it
Can now do nothing
By suffering.

All you lived through,
Dancing because you
No longer need it
For any deed.

I shall never be
Different. Love me.

3

O ear whose creatures cannot wish to fall,
O calm spaces unafraid of weight,
Where Sorrow is herself, forgetting all
The gaucheness of her adolescent state,
Where Hope within the altogether strange
From every outworn image is released,
And Dread born whole and normal like a beast
Into a world of truths that never change:
Restore our fallen day; O re-arrange.

O dear white children casual as birds,
Playing among the ruined languages,
So small beside their large confusion words,
So gay against the greater silences
Of dreadful things you did: O hang the head,
Impetuous child with the tremendous brain,
O weep, child, weep, O weep away the stain,
Lost innocence who wished your lover dead,
Weep for the lives your wishes never led.

O cry created as the bow of sin
Is drawn across our trembling violin.
O weep, child, weep, O weep away the stain.
O law drummed out by hearts against the still
Long winter of our intellectual will.
That what has been may never be again,
O flute that throbs with the thanksgiving breath
Of convalescents on the shores of death.
O bless the freedom that you never chose.
O trumpets that unguarded children blow
About the fortress of their inner foe.
O wear your tribulation like a rose.

Ode to Gaea

From this new culture of the air we finally see,
Far-shining in excellence, what our Mother, the
        Nicest daughter of Chaos, would
      Admire could she look in a glass,

And what, in her eyes, is natural: it is the old
Grand style of gestures we watch as, heavy with cold,
        The top-waters of all her
      Northern seas take their vernal plunge,

And suddenly her desolations, salt as blood,
Prolix yet terse, are glamorously carpeted
        With great swatches of plankton,
      Delicious spreads of nourishment,

While, in her realm of solids, lively dots expand,
Companionship becomes an unstaid passion and
        Leaves by the mile hide tons of
      Pied pebbles that will soon be birds.

Now that we know how she looks, she seems more mysterious
Than when, in her *partibus infidelibus*,
        We painted sizzling dragons
      And wizards reading upside down,

But less approachable: where she joins girl's-ear lakes
To bird's-foot deltas with lead-blue squiggles she makes,
        Surely, a value judgement,
      'Of pure things Water is the best,'

But how does she rank wheelwrights? One doubts if she knows
Which sub-species of folly is peculiar to those
        Pretty molehills, where on that
      Pocket-handkerchief of a plain

The syntax changes: peering down sleepily at
A crenellated shore, the tired old diplomat
        Becomes embarrassed – Should he
      Smile for 'our great good ally', scowl

At 'that vast and detestable empire' or choose
The sneer reserved for certain Southern countries 'whose
        Status and moral climate
      We have no desire, sir, to emulate'?

But why should we feel neglected on mountain drives,
Unpopular in woods, is quite clear; the older lives
        Have no wish to be stood in
      Rows or at right angles: below

Straight as its railroads, cutting diagonally across
A positivist republic, two lines of moss
        Show where the Devil's Causeway
      Drew pilgrims seven gods ago,

And on this eve of whispers and tapped telephones
Before the Ninth Catastrophe, square corner-stones
        Still distinguish a fortress
      Of the High Kings from untutored rock.

Tempting to mortals in the fancy of half-concerned
Gods in the sky, of a bored Thunderer who turned
        From the Troy-centred grief to
      Watch the Hippemolgoi drink their milk,

And how plausible from his look-point: we may well
Shake a weak fist one day at this vision, but the spell
        Of high places will haunt us
      Long after our jaunt has declined,

As soon it must, to the hard ground. Where six foot is tall,
Good-manners will ask easy riddles like 'Why are all

The rowdiest marches and the
Most venomous iambics composed

By lame clergymen?', will tell no tales which end in worse
Disaster than that of the tipsy poet who cursed
        A baby for whom later
    He came to sigh – so we were taught

Before the Greater Engines came and the police
Who go with them, when the long rivers ran through peace
        And the holy laws of Speech were
    Held in awe, even by evil tongues,

And manners, maybe, will stand us in better stead,
Down there, than a kantian conscience; from overhead
        Much harm is discernible,
    Farms unroofed and harbour-works wrecked

In the Second Assault; frank to an ungrieving sky
As still they look, too many fertilities lie
        In dread of the tormentor's
    Fondling finger, and in the few

That still have poky shops and audiences of one,
Many are overweight, the pious peasant's only son,
        Goading their crumpled faces
    Down innocence-corrupting roads,

Dreams of cities where his cows are whores. When the wise
Wilt in the glare of the Shadow, the stern advise
        Tribute and the large-hearted
    Already talk Its gibberish,

Perhaps a last stand in the passes will be made
By those whose Valhalla would be hearing verse by Praed
        Or arias by Rossini
    Between two entrées by Careme.

We hope so. But who on Cupid's Coming would car
More than one World's Bane has been scotched before t
      Justice during his *Te Deum*
    Slipped away sighing from the hero's pew,

And Earth, till the end, will be herself; she has never been moved
Except by Amphion, and orators have not improved
      Since misled Athens perished
    Upon Sicilian marble: what,

To her, the real one, can our good landscapes be but lies,
Those woods where tigers chum with deer and no root dies,
      That tideless bay where children
    Play bishop on a golden shore.

The Shield of Achilles

    She looked over his shoulder
      For vines and olive trees,
    Marble well-governed cities
      And ships upon untamed seas,
    But there on the shining metal
      His hands had put instead
    An artificial wilderness
      And a sky like lead.

A plain without a feature, bare and brown,
    No blade of grass, no sign of neighbourhood,
Nothing to eat and nowhere to sit down,
    Yet, congregated on its blankness, stood
    An unintelligible multitude.
A million eyes, a million boots in line,
Without expression, waiting for a sign.

f the air a voice without a face
roved by statistics that some cause was just
In tones as dry and level as the place:
    No one was cheered and nothing was discussed;
    Column by column in a cloud of dust
They marched away enduring a belief
Whose logic brought them, somewhere else, to grief.

    She looked over his shoulder
        For ritual pieties,
    White flower-garlanded heifers,
        Libation and sacrifice,
    But there on the shining metal
        Where the altar should have been,
    She saw by his flickering forge-light
        Quite another scene.

Barbed wire enclosed an arbitrary spot
    Where bored officials lounged (one cracked a joke)
And sentries sweated for the day was hot:
    A crowd of ordinary decent folk
    Watched from without and neither moved nor spoke
As three pale figures were led forth and bound
To three posts driven upright in the ground.

The mass and majesty of this world, all
    That carries weight and always weighs the same
Lay in the hands of others; they were small
    And could not hope for help and no help came:
    What their foes liked to do was done, their shame
Was all the worst could wish; they lost their pride
And died as men before their bodies died.

    She looked over his shoulder
        For athletes at their games
    Men and women in a dance
        Moving their sweet limbs
    Quick, quick, to music,

But there on the shining shield
His hands had set no dancing-floor
But a weed-choked field.

A ragged urchin, aimless and alone,
    Loitered about that vacancy, a bird
Flew up to safety from his well-aimed stone:
    That girls are raped, that two boys knife a third,
    Were axioms to him, who'd never heard
Of any world where promises were kept,
Or one could weep because another wept.

The thin-lipped armourer,
    Hephaestos hobbled away,
Thetis of the shining breasts
    Cried out in dismay
At what the god had wrought
    To please her son, the strong
Iron-hearted man-slaying Achilles
    Who would not live long.

JOHN BETJEMAN

Upper Lambourne

Up the ash-tree climbs the ivy,
    Up the ivy climbs the sun,
With a twenty-thousand pattering
    Has a valley breeze begun,
Feathery ash, neglected elder,
    Shift the shade and make it run —

Shift the shade toward the nettles,
    And the nettles set it free
To streak the stained Cararra headstone
    Where, in nineteen-twenty-three,
He who trained a hundred winners
    Paid the Final Entrance Fee.

Leathery limbs of Upper Lambourne,
    Leathery skin from sun and wind,
Leathery breeches, spreading stables,
    Shining saddles left behind —
To the down the string of horses
    Moving out of sight and mind.

Feathery ash in leathery Lambourne
    Waves above the sarsen stone,
And Edwardian plantations
    So coniferously moan
As to make the swelling downland
    Far-surrounding, seem their own.

Bristol

Green upon the flooded Avon shone the after-storm-wet sky
Quick the struggling withy branches let the leaves of autumn fly
And a star shone over Bristol, wonderfully far and high.

Ringers in an oil-lit belfry – Britton? Kelston? who shall say? –
Smoothly practising a plain course, caverned out the dying day
As their melancholy music flooded up and ebbed away.

Then all Somerset was round me and I saw the clippers ride,
High above the moonlit houses, triple-masted on the tide,
By the tall embattled church-towers of the Bristol waterside.

And an undersong to branches dripping into pools and wells
Out of multitudes of elm trees over leagues of hills and dells
Was the mathematic pattern of a plain course on the bells.*

```
*1 2 2 4 4 5 5 3 3 1 1
 2 1 4 2 5 4 3 5 1 3 2
 3 4 1 5 2 3 4 1 5 2 3
 4 3 5 1 3 2 1 4 2 5 4
 5 5 3 3 1 1 2 2 4 4 5
```

Youth and Age on Beaulieu River, Hants

Early sun on Beaulieu water
    Lights the undersides of oaks,
Clumps of leaves it floods and blanches,
All transparent glow the branches
    Which the double sunlight soaks;
To her craft on Beaulieu water
Clemency the General's daughter
    Pulls across with even strokes.

Schoolboy-sure she is this morning;
    Soon her sharpie's rigg'd and free.
Cool beneath a garden awning
    Mrs Fairclough, sipping tea
And raising large long-distance glasses
As the little sharpie passes,
    Sighs our sailor girl to see:

Tulip figure, so appealing,
 Oval face, so serious-eyed,
Tree-roots pass'd and muddy beaches.
On to huge and lake-like reaches,
 Soft and sun-warm, see her glide –
Slacks the slim young limbs revealing,
Sun-brown arm the tiller feeling –
 With the wind and with the tide.

Evening light will bring the water,
 Day-long sun will burst the bud,
Clemency, the General's daughter,
 Will return upon the flood.
But the older woman only
Knows the ebb-tide leaves her lonely
 With the shining fields of mud.

I. M.
Walter Ramsden
Ob. March 26, 1947,
Pembroke College, Oxford

Dr. Ramsden cannot read *The Times* obituary to-day,
 He's dead.
Let monographs on silk worms by other people be
 Thrown away
 Unread
For he who best could understand and criticize them, he
 Lies clay
 In bed.

The body waits in Pembroke College where the ivy taps the panes
 All night;
That old head so full of knowledge, that good heart that kept the
 brains
 All right,

Those old cheeks that faintly flushed as the port suffused the veins,
            Drain'd white.

Crocus in the Fellows' Garden, winter jasmine up the wall
            Gleam gold.
Shadows of Victorian chimneys on the sunny grassplot fall
            Long, cold.
Master, Bursar, Senior Tutor, these, his three survivors, all
            Feel old.

They remember, as the coffin to its final obsequations
            Leaves the gates,
Buzz of bees in window boxes on their summer ministrations,
            Kitchen din,
            Cups and plates,
And the getting of bump suppers for the long-dead generations
            Coming in,
            From Eights.

NORMAN CAMERON

Forgive Me, Sire

Forgive me, Sire, for cheating your intent,
That I, who should command a regiment,
Do amble amiably here, O God,
One of the neat ones in your awkward squad.

Three Love Poems

FROM A WOMAN TO A GREEDY LOVER

What is this recompense you'd have from me?
Melville asked no compassion of the sea.
Roll to and fro, forgotten in my wrack,
Love as you please – I owe you nothing back.

IN THE QUEEN'S ROOM

In smoky outhouses of the court of love
I chattered, a recalcitrant underling
Living on scraps. 'Below stairs or above,
All's one,' I said. 'We valets have our fling.'

Now I am come, by a chance beyond reach,
Into your room, my body smoky and soiled
And on my tongue the taint of chattering speech,
Tell me, Queen, am I irredeemably spoiled?

SHEPHERDESS

All day my sheep have mingled with yours. They strayed
Into your valley seeking a change of ground.
Held and bemused with what they and I had found,
Pastures and wonders, heedlessly I delayed.

Now it is late. The tracks leading home are steep,
The stars and landmarks in your country are strange.
How can I take my sheep back over the range?
Shepherdess, show me now where I may sleep.

The Firm of Happiness, Limited

The firm of Happiness, Limited, was one to astonish the stars,
More like a thriving town than a multiple store – a hotchpotch
Of markets and playrooms and chapels and brothels and baths and
    bars,
As smoothly running and closely packed as the works of a watch.

Nobody finally understood the cause of the crash.
Some spoke of Nemesis; others rumoured, vaguely, of course,
That a gang of Directors had simply robbed the firm of its cash,
Or that some ironical Jew was selling it short on the Bourse.

Whatever the reason, the firm of a sudden began to fail.
The floors were undusted at corners, the commissionaires were
    unshaved,
The girls were anxious and raucous, the comedian's jokes were stale.
The customers noticed the difference – to judge from the way they
    behaved.

When Happiness closed its doors, the Corporation of the city
Were distressed to see so vast a property left alone
To moulder and waste; in a mingled impulse of thrift and pity
They decided to buy the empty building, and floated a loan.

Now nobody knows what to do with this monstrous hulk we have
    bought.
At the last Corporation meeting one alderman, half in jest,
Spoke of turning it into a barracks. Meanwhile there's the dreary
    thought
That we ratepayers have to keep paying the burdensome interest.

Green, Green is El Aghir

Sprawled on the crates and sacks in the rear of the truck,
I was gummy-mouthed from the sun and the dust of the track,
And the two Arab soldiers I'd taken on as hitch-hikers
At a torrid petrol-dump, had been there on their hunkers
Since early morning. I said, in a kind of French
'On m'a dit, qu'il y a une belle source d'eau fraîche,
Plus loin, à El Aghir' . . .
                         It was eighty more kilometres
Until round a corner we heard a splashing of waters,
And there, in a green, dark street, was a fountain with two faces
Discharging both ways, from full throated faucets
Into basins, thence into troughs and thence into brooks.
Our negro corporal driver slammed his brakes,
And we yelped and leapt from the truck and went at the double
To fill our bidons and bottles and drink and dabble.
Then, swollen with water, we went to an inn for wine.
The Arabs came, too, though their faith might have stood between.
'After all,' they said, 'it's a boisson,' without contrition.

Green, green is El Aghir. It has a railway-station,
And the wealth of its soil has born many another fruit,
A mairie, a school and an elegant Salle de Fêtes.
Such blessings, as I remarked, in effect, to the waiter,
Are added unto them that have plenty of water.

ROY CAMPBELL

Luis de Camões

Camões, alone, of all the lyric race,
Born in the black aurora of disaster,
Can look a common soldier in the face:
I find a comrade where I sought a master:
For daily, while the stinking crocodiles
Glide from the mangroves on the swampy shore,
He shares my awning on the dhow, he smiles,
And tells me that he lived it all before.
Through fire and shipwreck, pestilence and loss,
Led by the ignis fatuus of duty
To a dog's death – yet of his sorrows king –
He shouldered high his voluntary Cross,
Wrestled his hardships into forms of beauty,
And taught his gorgon destinies to sing.

En Una Noche Oscura
Translated from St John of the Cross

Upon a gloomy night,
With all my cares to loving ardours flushed,
(O venture of delight!)
With nobody in sight
I went abroad when all the house was hushed.

In safety, in disguise,
In darkness, up the secret stair I crept,
(O happy enterprise!)
Concealed from other eyes
When all my home at length in silence slept.

Upon that lucky night,
In secrecy, inscrutable to sight,
I went without discerning
And with no other light
Except for that which in my heart was burning.

It lit and led me through,
More certain than the light of noonday clear,
To where One waited near
Whose presence well I knew,
There, where no other presence might appear.

O Night that was my guide!
O Darkness dearer than the morning's pride,
O Night that joined the lover
To the beloved bride,
Transfiguring them each into the other!

Within my flowering breast,
Which only for himself entire I save,
He sank into his rest
And all my gifts I gave,
Lulled by the airs with which the cedars wave.

Over the ramparts fanned,
While the fresh wind was fluttering his tresses,
With his serenest hand
My neck he wounded, and
Suspended every sense in its caresses.

Lost to myself I stayed,
My face upon my lover having laid
From all endeavour ceasing:
And, all my cares releasing,
Threw them amongst the lilies there to fade.

November Nights

On the westmost point of Europe, where it blows with might and
    main,
While loudly on the village-spires the weathercocks are shrieking,
And gusty showers, like kettledrums, are rattled on the pane,
The rafters like the shrouds of some old sailing-ship are creaking,
And the building reels and rumbles as it rides the wind and rain.

The treetops clash their antlers in their ultimate dishevelry:
The combers crash along the cliffs to swell the dreadful revelry,
And to the nightlong blaring of the lighthouse on the rocks
The fog-horns of the ships reply. The wolves in all their devilry,
Starved out of the sierras, have been slaughtering the flocks.

Now peasants shun the muddy fields, and fisherfolk the shores.
It is the time the weather finds the wounds of bygone wars,
And never to a charger did I take as I have done
To cantering the rocking-chair, my Pegasus, indoors,
For my olives have been gathered and my grapes are in the tun.

Between the gusts the wolves raise up a long-drawn howl of woe:
The mastiff whines, with bristled hair, beside us cowering low,
But for the firelight on your face I would not change the sun,
Nor would I change a moment of our winter-season, no,
For our springtime with its orioles and roses long ago.

WILLIAM EMPSON

Autumn on Nan-Yueh

(With the exiled universities of Peking)

> *The soul remembering its loneliness*
> *Shudders in many cradles . . .*
> *. . . soldier, honest wife by turns,*
> *Cradle within cradle, and all in flight, and all*
> *Deformed because there is no deformity*
> *But saves us from a dream.*
>
> W. B. Yeats

If flight's as general as this
    And every movement starts a wing
('Turn but a stone,' the poet found
    Winged angels crawling that could sting),
Eagles by hypothesis
    And always taking a new fling,
Scorners eternal of the ground
    And all the rocks where one could cling,
We obviously give a miss
    To earth and all that kind of thing,
And cart our Paradise around
    Or all that footless birds can bring.

I have flown here, part of the way,
    Being air-minded where I must
(The Victorian train supplies a bed;
    Without it, where I could, I bussed),
But here for quite a time I stay
    Acquiring moss and so forth – rust,
And it is true, I flew, I fled,
    I ran about on hope, on trust,
I felt I had escaped from They
    Who sat on pedestals and fussed.

But is it true one ought to dread
    This timid flap, that shirk, that lust?
We do not fly when we are clay.
    We hope to fly when we are dust.

The holy mountain where I live
    Has got some bearing on the Yeats.
Sacred to Buddha, and a god
    Itself, it straddles the two fates;
And has deformities to give
    You dreams by all its paths and gates.
They may be dreamless. It is odd
    To hear them yell out jokes and hates
And pass the pilgrims through a sieve,
    Brought there in baskets or in crates.
The pilgrims fly because they plot.
    The topmost abbot has passed Greats.

'The soul remembering' is just
    What we professors have to do.
(The souls aren't lonely now; this room
    Beds four and as I write holds two.
They shudder at the winter's thrust
    In cradles that encourage 'flu.)
The abandoned libraries entomb
What all the lectures still go through,
And men get curiously non-plussed
    Searching the memory for a clue.
The proper Pegasi to groom
    Are those your mind is willing to.
Let textual variants be discussed;
    We teach a poem as it grew.

Remembering prose is quite a trouble
    But of Mrs Woolf one tatter
Many years have failed to smother.
    As a piece of classroom patter

47

It would not repay me double.
 Empire builder reads the yatter
In one monthly, then another:
 'Thank God I left' (this is my smatter)
'That pernicious hubble-bubble
 If only to hear baboons chatter
And coolies beat their wives.' A brother
 I feel and it is me I flatter.

They say the witches thought they flew
 Because some drug made them feel queer.
There is exorbitance enough
 And a large broomstick in plain beer.
As for the Tiger Bone, the brew
 With roses we can still get here,
The village brand is coarse and rough,
 And the hot water far from clear.
It makes a grog. It is not true
 That only an appalling fear
Would drive a man to drink the stuff.
 Besides you do not drink to steer
Far out away into the blue.
 The chaps use drink for getting near.

Verse has been lectured to a treat
 Against escape and being blah.
It struck me trying not to fly
 Let them escape a bit too far.
It is an aeronautic feat
 Called soaring, makes you quite a star
(The Queen and Alice did) to try
 And keep yourself just where you are.
But who was bold enough to meet
 Exactly who on Phoebus' car
Slung on a Blimp to be a spy
 I ask before I cry Hurrah?

I pushed the Yeats up to the top
    Feeling it master of a flow
Of personal chat that would not end
    Without one root from which to grow.
That excellent poet's organ stop
    Has very wisely let us go
Just scolding all. He does not send
    Any advice so far below.
But yet this Dream, that's such a flop,
    As all the latest people know,
He makes no leak we ought to mend
    Or gas-escape that should not blow,
But what they fly from, whence they drop,
    The truth that they forsake for show.

Besides, I really do not like
    The verses about 'Up the Boys,'
The revolutionary romp,
    The hearty uproar that deploys
A sit-down literary strike;
    The other curly-headed toy's
The superrealistic comp.
    By a good student who enjoys
A nightmare handy as a bike.
    You find a cluster of them cloys.
But all conventions have their pomp
    And all styles can come down to noise.

Indeed I finally agree
    You do in practice have to say
This crude talk about Escape
    Cannot be theorised away.
Yeats is adroit enough to see
    His old word Dream must now leave play
For dreams in quite another shape,
    And Freud, and that his word can stay.

That force and breadth of mind all we
    Can't hope for, whether bleak or gay;
We put his soundings down on tape
    And mark where others went astray.
So dreams it may be right to flee,
    And as to fleeing, that we may.

So far I seem to have forgot
    About the men who really soar.
We think about them quite a bit;
    Elsewhere there's reason to think more.
With Ministers upon the spot
    (Driven a long way from the War)
And training camps, the place is fit
    For bombs. The railway was the chore
Next town. The thing is, they can not
    Take aim. Two hundred on one floor
Were wedding guests cleverly hit
    Seven times and none left to deplore.

Politics are what verse should
    Not fly from, or it goes all wrong.
I feel the force of that all right,
    And had I speeches they were song.
But really, does it do much good
    To put in verse however strong
The welter of a doubt at night
    At home, in which I too belong?
The heat-mists that my vision hood
    Shudder precisely with the throng.
England I think an eagle flight
    May come too late, may take too long.
What would I teach it? Where it could
    The place has answered like a gong.

What are these things I do not face,
    The reasons for entire despair,

Trenching the map into the lines
    That prove no building can be square?
Not nationalism nor yet race
    Poisons the mind, poisons the air,
Excuses, consequences, signs,
    But not the large thing that is there.
Real enough to keep a place
    Like this from owning its new heir;
But economics are divines,
    They have the floor, they have the flair. ....

Revolt and mercy fired no sparks
    In the Red argument at all;
Only what all of us desire,
    That the whole system should not stall.
The real impressiveness of Marx
    Lay in combining a high call
With what seemed proof that certain fire
    Attended all who joined with Saul.
Stalin amended his remarks
    By saying they would not fall
But must be trod into the mire
    (And till his baby state could crawl
It must not venture on such larks).
    This let them back against a wall.

The tedious triumphs of the mind
    Are more required than some suppose
To make a destiny absurd
    And dung a desert for a rose.
It seems unpleasantly refined
    To put things off till someone knows.
Economists have got the bird
    And dignity and high repose.
One asked me twenty years to find
    The thread to where the monster grows.

But we wait upon the word
  They may too late or not disclose.

'This passive style might pass perhaps
  Squatting in England with the beer.
But if that's all you think of, what
  In God's name are you doing here?
If economics sent the Japs
  They have the rudder that will steer;
Pretence of sympathy is not
  So rare it pays you for a tear.
Hark at these Germans, hopeful chaps,
  Who mean to split the country dear.'
It is more hopeful on the spot.
  The 'News', the conferences that leer,
The creeping fog, the civil traps,
  These are what force you into fear.

Besides, you aren't quite good for nowt
  Or clinging wholly as a burr
Replacing men who must get out,
  Nor is it shameful to aver
A vague desire to be about
  Where the important things occur . . .
And no desire at all to tout
  About how blood strokes down my fur –
We have a Pandarus school of trout
  That hangs round battles just to purr –
The Golden Bough, you needn't doubt,
  'Are crucifixions what they were?' . . .

I said I wouldn't fly again
  For quite a bit. I did not know.
Even in breathing tempest-tossed,
  Scattering to winnow and to sow,
With convolutions for a brain,

Man moves, and we have got to go.
Claiming no heavy personal cost
I feel the poem would be slow
Furtively finished on the plain.
We have had the autumn here. But oh
That lovely balcony is lost
Just as the mountains take the snow.
The soldiers will come here and train.
The streams will chatter as they flow.

ROBERT GRAVES

A Plea to Boys and Girls

You learned Lear's *Nonsense Rhymes* by heart, not rote;
    You learned Pope's *Iliad* by rote, not heart;
These terms should be distinguished if you quote
    My verses, children – keep them poles apart –
And call the man a liar who says I wrote
    All that I wrote in love, for love of art.

Dialogue on the Headland

SHE: You'll not forget these rocks and what I told you?
HE: How could I? Never: whatever happens.
SHE: What do you think might happen?
     Might you fall out of love? – did you mean that?
HE: Never, never! 'Whatever' was a sop
     For jealous listeners in the shadows.
SHE: You haven't answered me. I asked:
     'What do you think might happen?'
HE: Whatever happens: though the skies should fall
     Raining their larks and vultures in our laps –
SHE: 'Though the seas turn to slime' – say that –
     'Though water-snakes be hatched with six heads.'
HE: Though the seas turn to slime, or tower
     In an arching wave above us, three miles high –
SHE: 'Though she should break with you' – dare you say that? –
     'Though she deny her words on oath.'
HE: I had that in my mind to say, or nearly;
     It hurt so much I choked it back.
SHE: How many other days can't you forget?
     How many other loves and landscapes?
HE: You are jealous?
SHE: Damnably.

HE: The past is past.
SHE: And this?
HE: Whatever happens, this goes on.
SHE: Without a future? Sweetheart, tell me now:
       What do you want of me? I must know that.
HE: Nothing that isn't freely mine already.
SHE: Say what is freely yours and you shall have it.
HE: Nothing that, loving you, I should dare take.
SHE: O, for an answer with no 'nothing' in it!
HE: Then give me everything that's left.
SHE: Left after what?
HE: After whatever happens:
       Skies have already fallen, seas are slime,
       Watersnakes poke and peer six-headedly –
SHE: And I lie snugly in the Devil's arms.
HE: I said: 'Whatever happens.' Are you crying?
SHE: You'll not forget me – ever, ever, ever?

Beauty in Trouble

Beauty in trouble flees to the good angel
    On whom she can rely
To pay her cab-fare, run a steaming bath,
    Poultice her bruised eye;

Will not at first, whether for shame or caution,
    Her difficulty disclose;
Until he draws a cheque book from his plumage,
    Asking her how much she owes.

(Breakfast in bed: coffee and marmalade,
    Toast, eggs, orange-juice,
After a long, sound sleep – the first since when? –
    And no word of abuse.)

Loves him less only than her saint-like mother,
　　Promises to repay
His loans and most seraphic thoughtfulness
　　A million-fold one day.

Beauty grows plump, renews her broken courage
　　And, borrowing ink and pen,
Writes a news-letter to the evil angel
　　(Her first gay act since when?)

The fiend who beats, betrays and sponges on her,
　　Persuades her white is black,
Flaunts vespertilian wing and cloven hoof;
　　And soon will fetch her back.

Virtue, good angel, is its own reward:
　　Your guineas were well spent.
But would you to the marriage of true minds
　　Admit impediment?

A Love Story

The full moon easterly rising, furious,
Against a winter sky ragged with red;
The hedges high in snow, and owls raving –
Solemnities not easy to withstand;
A shiver wakes the spine.

In boyhood, having encountered the scene,
I suffered horror: I fetched the moon home,
With owls and snow, to nurse in my head
Throughout the trials of a new Spring,
Famine unassuaged.

But fell in love, and made a lodgement
Of love on those chill ramparts.

Her image was my ensign: snows melted,
Hedges sprouted, the moon tenderly shone,
The owls trilled with tongues of nightingale.

These were all lies, though they matched the time,
And brought me less than luck: her image
Warped in the weather, turned beldamish.
Then back came winter on me at a bound,
The pallid sky heaved with a moon-quake.

Dangerous it had been with love-notes
To serenade Queen Famine.
In tears I recomposed the former scene,
Let the snow lie, watched the moon rise, suffered the owls,
Paid homage to them of unevent.

She Tells Her Love While Half Asleep

She tells her love while half asleep,
        In the dark hours,
                With half-words whispered low:
As Earth stirs in her winter sleep
                And puts out grass and flowers
                Despite the snow,
                Despite the falling snow.

1805

At Viscount Nelson's lavish funeral,
    While the mob milled and yelled about St Paul's,
A General chatted with an Admiral:

'One of your colleagues, Sir, remarked today
    That Nelson's *exit*, though to be lamented,
Falls not inopportunely, in its way.'

'He was a thorn in our flesh,' came the reply –
  'The most bird-witted, unaccountable,
Odd little runt that ever I did spy.

'One arm, one peeper, vain as Pretty Poll,
  A meddler, too, in foreign politics
And gave his heart in pawn to a plain moll.

'He would dare lecture us Sea Lords, and then
  Would treat his ratings as though men of honour
And play at leap-frog with his midshipmen!

'We tried to box him down, but up he popped,
  And when he'd banged Napoleon at the Nile
Became too much the hero to be dropped.

'You've heard that Copenhagen "blind eye" story?
  We'd tied him to Nurse Parker's apron-strings –
By G—d, he snipped them through and snatched the glory!'

'Yet,' cried the General, 'six-and-twenty sail
  Captured or sunk by him off Trafalgar –
That writes a handsome *finis* to the tale.'

'Handsome enough. The seas are England's now.
  That fellow's foibles need no longer plague us.
He died most creditably, I'll allow.'

'And, Sir, the secret of his victories?'
  'By his unServicelike, familiar ways, Sir,
He made the whole Fleet love him, damn his eyes!'

HUGH MACDIARMID

From IN MEMORIAM JAMES JOYCE
'Let the only consistency'

Let the only consistency
In the course of my poetry
Be like that of the hawthorn tree
Which in early Spring breaks
Fresh emerald, then by nature's law
Darkens and deepens and takes
Tints of purple-maroon, rose-madder and straw.

Sometimes these hues are found
Together, in pleasing harmony bound.
Sometimes they succeed each other. But through
All the changes in which the hawthorn is dight,
No matter in what order, one thing is sure
– The haws shine ever the more ruddily bright!
And when the leaves have passed
Or only in a few tatters remain
The tree to the winter condemned
                Stands forth at last
    Not bare and drab and pitiful,
But a candelabrum of oxidised silver gemmed
By innumerable points of ruby
Which dominate the whole and are visible
Even at a considerable distance
As flame-points of living fire.
That so it may be
With my poems too at last glance
Is my only desire.

All else must be sacrificed to this great cause.
I feel no hardships. I have counted the cost.
I with my heart's blood as the hawthorn with its haws
Which are sweetened and polished by the frost!

See how these haws burn, there down the drive,
In this autumn air that feels like cotton wool,
When the earth has a gelatinous limpness as a body dead as a whole
While its tissues are still alive!

Poetry is human existence come to life,
The glorious energy that once employed
Turns all else in creation null and void,
The flower and fruit, the meaning and goal,
Which won all else is needs removed by the knife
Even as a man who rises high
Kicks away the ladder he has come up by.

This single-minded zeal, this fanatic devotion to art
Is alien to the English poetic temperament no doubt,
'This narrowing intensity' as the English say,
But I have it, even as you had it, Yeats, my friend,
And would have it with me as with you at the end,
I who am infinitely more un-English than you
And turn Scotland to poetry like those women who
In their passion secrete and turn to
Musk through and through!

So I think of you, Joyce, and of Yeats and others who are dead
As I walk this Autumn and observe
The birch tremulously pendulous in jewels of cairngorm,
The sauch, the osier, and the crack-willow
Of the beaten gold of Australia;
The sycamore in rich straw-gold;
The elm bowered in saffron;
The oak in flecks of salmon gold;
The beeches huge torches of living orange.

Billow on billow of autumnal foliage
From the sheer high bank glass themselves
Upon the ebon and silver current that floods freely
Past the shingle shelves.

I linger where a crack-willow slants across the stream,
Its olive leaves slashed with fine gold.
Beyond the willow a young beech
Blazes almost blood-red
Vying in intensity with the glowing cloud of crimson
That hangs about the purple bole of a gean
Higher up the brae face.

And yonder, the lithe green-grey bole of an ash, with its boughs
Draped in the cinnamon-brown lace of Samara.
(And I remember how in April on its bare twigs
The flowers came in ruffs like the unshorn ridges
Upon a French poodle – like a dull mulberry at first,
Before the first feathery fronds
Of the long-stalked, finely poised, seven-fingered leaves) –
Even the robin hushes its song
In these gold pavilions.

Other masters may conceivably write
Even yet in C major
But we – we take the perhaps 'primrose path'
To the dodecaphonic bonfire.

They are not endless, these variations of form
Though it is perhaps impossible to see them all.
It is certainly impossible to conceive one that does not exist.
But I keep trying in our forest to do both of these,
And though it is a long time now since I saw a new one
I am by no means weary yet of my concentration
On phyllotaxis here in preference to all else,
All else – but my sense of sny!

The gold edging of a bough at sunset, its pantile way
Forming a double curve, tegula and imbrex in one,
Seems at times a movement on which I might be borne
Happily to infinity; but again I am glad

When it suddenly ceases and I find myself
Pursuing no longer a rhythm of duramen
But bouncing on the diploe in a clearing between earth and air
Or headlong in dewy dallops or a moon-spairged fernshaw
Or caught in a dark dumosity, or even
In open country again watching an aching spargosis of stars.

'And above all, Karl Kraus'

And, above all, Karl Kraus
And his *Die Dritte Walpurgisnacht*
– Kraus whose thinking was a voyage
Of exploration in a landscape of words
And that language German
– For, while an English writer or speaker
Over long stretches of his verbal enterprise
Is protected by the tact and wisdom
Of linguistic convention, his German counterpart
Risks revealing himself as an idiot
Or a scoundrel through the ring and rhythm
Of his first sentence. Had Hitler's speeches
Been accessible to the West in their unspeakable original
We might have been spared the War
For the War was partly caused
By Hitler's innocent translators
Unavoidably missing in smooth and diplomatic
French or English the original's diabolic resonance.
Only German, in all its notorious long-windedness
Offers such short cuts to the termini of mankind.
It was Karl Kraus who knew them all.
He examined the language spoken and written
By his contemporaries and found
That they lived by wrong ideas.
Listening to what they said he discovered
The impure springs of their actions.
Reading what they wrote he knew
They were heading for disaster.

The linguistic structure of a diplomatic correspondent's report
Revealed more of the political situation
Than the conference so reported.
The diplomats may have had reason to be optimistic
But portents occurred in their reported speeches
– Wrong subjunctives and false inflections.
The hopes of the world
Proclaimed in manifestoes of good will
Came to grief at the barrier of a misplaced comma
And the highest expectations of mankind
Were frustrated by the verbal alliance with a cliché.
'The German language,' as he said,
'Is the profoundest of all languages,
But German speech is the shallowest.'

What was the inspiration of his vast productivity?
The answer is Hamlet's: 'Words, words, words!',
And the commas between them
And the deeds they beget
And the deeds they leave undone;
And the word that was at the beginning,
And, above all, the words that were at the end.
These were printed in newspapers.
Hence newspapers were one of his main themes;
And the men who wrote them,
And the things about which they wrote:
Society, law-courts, sex and morality,
Literature, theatre, war, commerce,
In brief the whole world that is called into being
By a headline, organised by a leading article,
And sold by an advertisement.
But his contrast theme was the words
That make up a drama by Shakespeare
Or a poem by Goethe.
Thus his theme behind the themes
Was the culture of Europe,

Its glory, its betrayal, its doom.
Exploring the labyrinths of contemporary verbiage
Karl Kraus never lost the thread,
His purpose 'to show the very age and body of the time
His form and pressure.'

Karl Kraus had an unfailing ear
For two kinds of sound: the common talk of the town
He satirically reproduced with amazing precision
And the language of prophecy he discerned
As the whispered accompaniment that, seemingly supporting
The trivial chat, suddenly forced it
Into a key of ultimate significance.
Oppressed by the confusing chorus of apparent triviality,
All the seething sciolism of the conventional world,
His ear was tuned to the pitch of the Absolute.
People gossiped about a War; he heard them
Lament the loss of their souls; at every street corner
Acts of high treason were committed.
The shouts of the newspaper boys
Announcing in mysterious vowels the latest edition
Became monstrous threats to man's spiritual safety,
Or cries of anguish from the lowest deep.
This metamorphosis of the commonplace will forever remain
One of the greatest achievements in the German language,
For the technique Karl Kraus employed,
If technique it was, was literal quotation;
The contrast was obtained
Not by a portentous raising of the voice
Or the use of prophetic diction
But simply by creating another context for the trivial.
He took the frivolous seriously, and discovered
The situation was desperate. His invention consisted
In assuming the existence of natural states of culture
And self-evidently correct norms of conduct;
For example – that modesty befits the mediocre –

And instantly mediocrity was seen
To have risen to demonic heights
From which it ruled the world.
He assumed that the prominent German writers and journalists
Of his time wrote in the German tongue
And the German tongue answered back
Saying they were illiterates.
He dealt with the practice of the law-courts
As though they were based on moral convictions,
With the theatre as though it were concerned
With the art of drama,
With journals as though they intended
To convey correct information,
With politicians as though they desired
The promotion of communal prosperity,
And with the philosophers as though
They were seekers after Truth.
The satirical effect of these inventions
Was annihilating.

His more important poetry is detached from his satire
Meeting it only at the source of their common inspiration,
The mystery of language.
A first and superficial judgement
May class the poetry as 'Epigonendichtung'
And that is what, in a particular sense,
He called it himself. Its forms, metres, rhythms and rhymes
Are traditional. It is determined
By the history of German poetry
From Goethe to Liliencron, yet bypasses the poet
Whose genius was to direct, and misdirect,
Distinctively modern trends – Hölderlin.
He had to remain outside Kraus's poetical orbit
For, with Hölderlin's later and greatest poems,
Poetry leaves its articulate German tradition,
Achieving the miracle of speechlessness

Bursting into speech.
If Goethe had the gift of his Tasso
To say what he suffered
And say it at a level of realisation
Where others would be silenced by agony,
Then Hölderlin sought,
And often miraculously found,
The word with which silence speaks
Its own silence without breaking it.

(Silence supervening at poetry's height,
Like the haemolytic streptococcus
In the sore throat preceding rheumatic fever
But which, at the height of the sickness,
Is no longer there, but has been and gone!
Or as 'laughter is the representative of tragedy
When tragedy is away.')

Short of miracles surpassing that miracle
From Hölderlin's poetry the way leads
Either to silence itself or to poetic mischief,
The verbose stammer of those who have never learned
To speak or to be silent,
Or the professional ecstasies of souls
That, only because they are uninhabitable,
Are constantly beside themselves.

'The world is fast bound in the snares of Varuna'

The world is fast bound in the snares of Varuna
– 'Cords consisting of serpents', according to Kulluka
(*Pasaih sarpa-rajjughih*). The winkings of men's eyes
Are all numbered by him; he wields the universe
As gamesters handle dice. These are the unexampled days
Of false witness – a barbarous régime which gives power over life
    and death

To an oligarchy of brigands and adventurers,
Without security from vexation by irresponsible tyrants,
Without protection of the home against the aggression of criminal
    bands,
Without impartial justice, without dignity.
We are denied all the deepest needs of men who do not wish
To sink to the level of the beasts – condemned
To a life deprived of its salt.

Already, everywhere,
The speed-up, the 'church work,' the lead poisoning,
The strain that drives men nuts.
The art of teaching fish by slow degrees
To live without water.
Men cheaper than safety
– Human relations have never sunk so low.
'The meaninglessness of the individual
Apart from his communal framework,'
The men in power who are worth no more
Than an equal number of cockroaches,
Unconcerned about values,
Indifferent to human quality
Or jealous and implacably hostile to it,
Full of the tyranny of coarse minds and degraded souls;
The abominable clap-trap and politicians' rhetoric,
The tawdry talk about the 'King' and 'the King's lieges'
And 'the Government' and 'the British people';
The concentration camps, the cat o' nine tails,
The law more lawless than any criminal,
The beatings-up by the police,
The countless thuggeries of Jacks-in-office,
The vile society women, infernal parasites,
The endless sadism, Gorilla-rule,
The live men hanging in the plaza
With butcher's hooks through their jaws
– And everywhere the worship of 'efficiency,'

Of whatever 'works' no matter to what ends,
The general feeling that if a thing
'Runs like a machine' it is all right
– That there can be no higher praise;
Mechanical authoritarianism,
A Lord Lloyd thinking 'the whole method of conference
Adverse to efficient government'
– Those (as Leonard Woolf has said)
Who question the authority of the machine,
Who claim the right to do what they want
And to be governed by themselves,
Condemned as rebels and extremists
Against whose claims to freedom of soul
It is the primary duty of all loyal citizens
To vindicate the machinery of law and order
– Against the claims of
Aminu Kano in Nigeria,
Cheddi Jagan in 'British' Guiana,
Liam Kelly and the Fianna Uladh in Northern Ireland.

But if, as could be, ninety per cent
Of human drudgery were abolished tomorrow
And the great masses of mankind given
Ample incomes and freed for 'higher things'
They could no more live than fish out of water,
They could not sustain life on that level
– On any level worthy of Man at all.

The ancestors of oysters and barnacles had heads.
Snakes have lost their limbs
And ostriches and penguins their power of flight.
Man may just as easily lose his intelligence.
Most of our people already have.
It is unlikely that man will develop into anything higher.
Unless he desires to and is prepared to pay the cost.
Otherwise we shall go the way of the dodo and the kiwi.

Already that process seems far advanced.
Genius is becoming rarer,
Our bodies a little weaker in each generation,
Culture is slowly declining,
Mankind is returning to barbarism
And will finally become extinct.

LOUIS MACNEICE

Brother Fire

When our brother Fire was having his dog's day
Jumping the London streets with millions of tin cans
Clanking at his tail, we heard some shadow say
'Give the dog a bone' – and so we gave him ours;
Night after night we watched him slaver and crunch away
The beams of human life, the tops of topless towers.

Which gluttony of his for us was Lenten fare
Who mother-naked, suckled with sparks, were chill
Though cotted in a grill of sizzling air
Striped like a convict – black, yellow and red;
Thus were we weaned in a knowledge of the Will
That wills the natural world but wills us dead.

O delicate walker, babbler, dialectician Fire,
O enemy and image of ourselves,
Did we not on those mornings after the All Clear,
When you were looting shops in elemental joy
And singing as you swarmed up city block and spire,
Echo your thought in ours? 'Destroy! Destroy!'

EDWIN MUIR

The Annunciation

The angel and the girl are met.
Earth was the only meeting place.
For the embodied never yet
Travelled beyond the shore of space.
The eternal spirits in freedom go.

See, they have come together, see,
While the destroying minutes flow,
Each reflects the other's face
Till heaven in hers and earth in his
Shine steady there. He's come to her
From far beyond the farthest star,
Feathered through time. Immediacy
Of strangest strangeness is the bliss
That from their limbs all movement takes.
Yet the increasing rapture brings
So great a wonder that it makes
Each feather tremble on his wings.

Outside the window footsteps fall
Into the ordinary day
And with the sun along the wall
Pursue their unreturning way
That was ordained in eternity.
Sound's perpetual roundabout
Rolls its numbered octaves out
And hoarsely grinds its battered tune.

But through the endless afternoon
These neither speak nor movement make,
But stare into their deepening trance
As if their gaze would never break.

Orpheus' Dream

And she was there. The little boat,
Coasting the perilous isles of sleep,
Zones of oblivion and despair,
Stopped, for Eurydice was there.
The foundering skiff could scarcely keep
All that felicity afloat.

As if we had left earth's frontier wood
Long since and from this sea had won
The lost original of the soul,
The moment gave us pure and whole
Each back to each, and swept us on
Past every choice to boundless good.

Forgiveness, truth, atonement, all
Our love at once – till we could dare
At last to turn out heads and see
The poor ghost of Eurydice
Still sitting in her silver chair,
Alone in Hades' empty hall.

The Child Dying

Unfriendly friendly universe,
I pack your stars into my purse,
And bid you, bid you so farewell.
That I can leave you, quite go out,
Go out, go out beyond all doubt,
My father says, is the miracle.

You are so great, and I so small:
I am nothing, you are all:
Being nothing, I can take this way.

Oh I need neither rise nor fall,
For when I do not move at all
I shall be out of all your day.

It's said some memory will remain
In the other place, grass in the rain,
Light on the land, sun on the sea,
A flitting grace, a phantom face,
But the world is out. There is no place
Where it and its ghosts can ever be.

Father, father, I dread this air
Blown from the far side of despair,
The cold cold corner. What house, what hold,
What hand is there? I look and see
Nothing-filled eternity,
And the great round world grows weak and old.

Hold my hand, oh hold it fast –
I am changing! – until at last
My hand in yours no more will change,
Though yours change on. You here, I there,
So hand in hand, twin-leafed despair –
I did not know death was so strange.

WILLIAM PLOMER

Sounds of Pleasure: Cannes, 1938

The Mediterranean sighs
   Because it is so calm:
On an evening such as this
   The rustling of a palm
Seems almost ominous,
   Whispering of nemesis.

Frenchmen there are who warn
   Divided France
Of doom to come –
   Come now, it's time to dance,
The hives are full of drones,
   Hotels begin to hum.

The hissing of a crowded lift
   Going down,
The clashing open of the gate,
   The frou-frou of a gown,
High heels in a light tattoo
   Tapping to keep a date.

From the tilted bottle
   Comes the gay
Chuckle of the happiest drink:
   Cast care away!
In the glass the bubbles seethe;
   Lifted glasses clink.

Click like castanets
   The excited dentures
Of the holder of a packet
   Of twelve per cent debentures:

For another year or two
   He can stand the racket.

Powdered arms and tinted nails
   Functioning like cranes
Sweep a wise man off his feet –
   Tonight a Princess entertains
The great Sir Mucous Membrane,
   Doyen of Harley Street.

Two exiled Kings,
   Fellow impotentates,
Dine with a diseuse
   Who cachinnates:
Oh, had their wits been half
   As quick as hers!

Loudly the rich obscure
   Applaud the Cuban band.
A rhumba oils the knees
   Of the would-be grand,
And in a narrow space
   They shuffle and squeeze.

Count Lausig, who would sell
   His granny if he could,
Dances with Violet Ray
   Over from Hollywood,
And there is Susan Trout,
   Sixty, if she's a day.

The rich, how rich they smell!
   Their jewels glint like stars,
Splendid, like plunder,
   Fragrant like cigars,
Love-gods and goddesses they love –
   Do they? I wonder.

The sibilance of dancing feet
  Where dancing is in fashion,
The labial of a kiss,
  The gutturals of passion:
Worldlings, remember all these sounds,
  They'll be an end to this.

The Mediterranean sighs
  Because it is so calm:
On an evening such as this
  The rustling of a palm
Seems almost ominous,
  Whispering of nemesis.

STEVIE SMITH

Not Waving But Drowning

Nobody heard him, the dead man,
But still he lay moaning:
I was much further out than you thought
And not waving but drowning.

Poor chap, he always loved larking
And now he's dead
It must have been too cold for him his heart gave way,
They said.

Oh, no no no, it was too cold always
(Still the dead one lay moaning)
I was much too far out all my life
And not waving but drowning.

Away, Melancholy

Away, melancholy,
Away with it, let it go.

Are not the trees green,
The earth as green?
Does not the wind blow,
Fire leap and the rivers flow?
Away melancholy.

The ant is busy
He carrieth his meat,
All things hurry
To be eaten or eat.
Away, melancholy.

Man, too, hurries,
Eats, couples, buries,
He is an animal also
With a hey ho melancholy,
Away with it, let it go.

Man of all creatures
Is superlative
(Away melancholy)
He of all creatures alone
Raiseth a stone
(Away melancholy)
Into the stone, the god
Pours what he knows of good
Calling, good, God.
Away melancholy, let it go.

Speak not to me of tears,
Tyranny, pox, wars,
Saying, Can God
Stone of man's thought, be good?
Say rather it is enough
That the stuffed
Stone of man's good, growing,
By man's called God.
Away, melancholy, let it go.

Man aspires
To good,
To love
Sighs;

Beaten, corrupted, dying
In his own blood lying
Yet heaves up an eye above
Cries, Love, love.
It is his virtue needs explaining,
Not his failing.

Away, melancholy,
Away with it, let it go.

My Heart Goes Out

My heart goes out to my Creator in love
Who gave me Death, as end and remedy.
All living creatures come to quiet Death
For him to eat up their activity
And give them nothing, which is what they want although
When they are living they do not think so.

Songe D'Athalie
From Racine

It was a dream and shouldn't I bother about a dream?
But it goes on you know, tears me rather.
Of course I try to forget it but it will not let me.
Well it was on an extraordinarily dark night at midnight
My mother Queen Jezebel appeared suddenly before me
Looking just as she did the day she died, dressed grandly.
It was her pride you noticed, nothing she had gone through touched
    that
And she still had the look of being most carefully made up
She always made up a lot she didn't want people to know how old
    she was
She spoke: Be warned my daughter, true girl to me, she said,
Do not suppose the cruel God of the Jews has finished with you,
I am come to weep your falling into his hands, my child.
With these appalling words my mother,
This ghost, leant over me stretching out her hands
And I stretched out my hands too to touch her
But what was it, oh this is horrible, what did I touch?
Nothing but the mangled flesh and the breaking bones
Of a body that the dogs tearing quarrelled over.

Childe Rolandine

Dark was the day for Childe Rolandine the artist
When she went to work as a secretary-typist
And as she worked she sang this song
Against oppression and the rule of wrong:

It is the privilege of the rich
To waste the time of the poor
To water with tears in secret
A tree that grows in secret
That bears fruit in secret
That ripened falls to the ground in secret
And manures the parent tree
Oh the wicked tree of hatred and the secret
The sap rising and the tears falling.

Likely also, sang the Childe, my soul will fry in hell
Because of this hatred, while in heaven my employer does well
And why should he not, exascerbating though he be but generous
Is it his fault I must work at a work that is tedious?
Oh heaven sweet heaven keep my thoughts in their night den
Do not let them by day be spoken.

But then she sang, Ah why not? tell all, speak, speak,
Silence is vanity, speak for the whole truth's sake.

And rising she took the bugle and put it to her lips, crying:
There is a Spirit feeds on our tears, I gave him mine,
Mighty human feelings are his food
Passion and grief and joy his flesh and blood
That he may live and grow fat we daily die   ·
This cropping One is our immortality.

Childe Rolandine bowed her head and in the evening
Drew the picture of the spirit from heaven.

Thoughts about the Person from Porlock

Coleridge received the Person from Porlock
And ever after called him a curse
Then why did he hurry to let him in?
He might have hid in the house.

It was not right of Coleridge in fact it was wrong
(But often we all do wrong)
As the truth is I think, he was already stuck
With Kubla Khan.

He was weeping and crying, I am finished, finished
I shall never write another word of it,
When along comes the Person from Porlock
And takes the blame for it.

It was not right it was wrong,
But often we all do wrong.

*

May we inquire the name of the Person from Porlock?
Why Porson, didn't you know?
He lived at the bottom of Porlock Hill
So had a long way to go.

He wasn't much in the social sense
Though his grandmother was a Warlock
One of the Rutlandshire ones I fancy
And nothing to do with Porlock.

But he lived at the bottom of a hill as I said
And had a cat named Flo
And had a cat named Flo.

*

I long for the Person from Porlock
To bring my thoughts to an end
I am becoming impatient to see him
I think of him as a friend

Often I look out of the window
Often I run to the gate
I think, He will come this evening
I think it is rather late.

I am hungry to be interrupted
For ever and ever amen
O Person from Porlock come quickly
And bring my thoughts to an end.

*

I felicitate the people who have a Person from Porlock
To break up everything and throw it away
Because then there will be nothing to keep them
And they need not stay.

*

Oh this Person from Porlock is a great interrupter
He interrupts us for ever
People say he is a dreadful fellow
But really he is desirable.

Why should they grumble so much?
He comes like a benison
They should be glad he has not forgotten them
They might have had to go on.

*

These thoughts are depressing, I know. They are depressing.
I wish I was more cheerful it is more pleasant
Also it is a duty, we should smile as well as submitting
To the purpose of One Above who is experimenting

With various mixtures of human character which goes best
All is interesting for him it is exciting, but not for us.
There I go again. Smile smile and get some work to do
Then you will be practically unconscious without positively having
    to go.

In the Park

Walking one day in the park in winter
I heard two silvered gentlemen talking,
Two old friends, elderly, walking, talking
There by the silver lake mid-pooled black in winter.

'Pray for the Mute who have no word to say,'
Cried one old gentleman, 'Not because they are dumb,
But they are weak. And the weak thoughts beating in the brain
Generate a sort of heat, yet cannot speak.
Thoughts that are bound without sound
In the tomb of the brain's room, wound. Pray for the Mute.'

'But' (said his friend), 'see how they swim
Free in the element best loved, so wet; yet breathe
As a visitor to the air come; plunge then, rejoicing more,
Having left it briefly for the visited shore, to come
Home to the wet
Windings that are yet
Best loved though familiar; and oh so right the wet
Stream and the wave; he is their pet.'
Finished, the mild friend
Smiled, put aside his well-tuned hearing instrument
And it seemed
The happiness he spoke of
Irradiated all his members, and his heart
Barked with delight to stress
So much another's happiness.

But which other's? The sombre first
Speaker reversed
The happy moment; cried again
(Mousing for pain) 'Pray for the Mute' (a tear drops)
'They are like the brute.'

Struck by the shout
That he may not know what it's about
The deaf friend again
Up-ends his hearing instrument to relieve the strain.
What? Oh shock, ' "Pray for the Mute"?
I thought you said the newt.'

Now which is Christianer pray, of these old friends, the one who
    will say
For pain's sake pray, pray; or the deaf other that rejoices
So much that the cool amphibian
Shall have his happiness, all things rejoicing with him?

But wait; the first speaker now, the old sombre one,
Is penetrated quite by his friend's sun
And, 'O blessed you,' he cries, 'to show
So in simplicity what is true.'
All his face is suffused with happy tears and he weeps as he sings a
    happy song,
Happier even than his friend's song was, righting the wrong.
So two, better than one, finally strike truth in this happy song:
'Praise,' cries the weeping softened one, 'Not pray, praise, all men,
Praise is the best prayer, the least self's there, that least's release.'

VERNON WATKINS

Swedenborg's Skull

Note this survivor, bearing the mark of the violator,
Yet still a vessel of uninterrupted calm.
Its converse is ended. They beat on the door of his coffin,
But they could not shake or destroy that interior psalm
Intended for God alone, for his sole Creator.
For gold they broke into his tomb.

The mark of the pick is upon him, that rough intrusion
Upon the threshold and still place of his soul.
With courtesy he received them. They stopped, astonished,
Where the senses had vanished, to see the dignified skull
Discoursing alone, entertaining those guests of his vision
Whose wit made the axe-edge dull.

Here the brain flashed its fugitive lightning, its secret appraising,
Where marble, settled in utmost composure, appears.
Here the heirs of the heavens were disposed in symmetrical orders
And a flash of perception transfigured the darkness of years.
The mark of a membrane is linked with those traffickers grazing
Its province of princes and spheres.

Where the robbers looked, meditations disputed the legacy
Of the dreaming mind, and the rungs of their commonplace crime
Gave way to swift places of angels, caught up in division
From the man upon earth; but his patience now played like a mime,
And they could not break down or interpret the skull in its privacy
Or take him away from his time.

So I see it today, the inscrutable mask of conception
Arrested in death. Hard, slender and grey, it transcends
The inquiring senses, even as a shell toiling inward,

Caught up from the waters of change by a traveller who bends
His piercing scrutiny, yields but a surface deception,
Still guarding the peace it defends.

The Feather

I stoop to gather a seabird's feather
Fallen on the beach,
Torn from a beautiful drifting wing;
What can I learn or teach,
Running my finger through the comb
And along the horny quill?
The body it was torn from
Gave out a cry so shrill,
Sailors looked from their white road
To see what help was there.
It dragged the winds to a drop of blood
Falling through drowned air,
Dropping from the sea-hawk's beak,
From frenzied talons sharp;
Now if the words they lost I speak
It must be to that harp
Under the strange, light-headed sea
That bears a straw of the nest.
Unless I make that melody,
How can the dead have rest?

Sheer from wide air to the wilderness
The victim fell, and lay;
The starlike bone is fathomless,
Lost among wind and spray.
This lonely, isolated thing
Trembles amid their sound.
I set my finger on the string
That spins the ages round.
But let it sleep, let it sleep

Where shell and stone are cast:
In ecstasy the Furies keep,
For nothing here is past.
The perfect into night must fly;
On this the winds agree.
How could a blind rock satisfy
The hungers of the sea?

Indolence

Count up those books whose pages you have read
Moulded by water. Wasps this paper made.
Come. You have taken tribute from the dead.
Your tribute to the quick must now be paid.

What lovelier tribute than to rest your head
Beneath this birchtree which is bound to fade?
And watch the branches quivering by a thread
Beyond interpretation of the shade.

The Death Bell
It tolls for *thee*. Donne

THE SUPPLICATION OF SILENCE

Hold fast the impatient bell
And let my soul have time
To count and ponder well
What steps he has to climb
To see what Simeon saw
And those three travelled kings,
Love that fulfils the law
Figured in limbs, not wings;
Whose hands uphold the throne
By that last promise given
That before day had gone

He'ld be with Him in heaven.
Pause, while I set my prayer
Against contending lust;
Then, on the doubting air
Give tongue, majestic dust.

For this bells tolls to birth
Him who hears: 'I, if I
Be lifted up from earth,
Will draw men unto Me.'
There in one height are met
Old age and swaddling-bands.
Before his life had set,
Simeon in his two hands
Caught up the babe, and praised
God, to a hidden lyre.
Love's resurrection blazed,
Changing, as by a fire,
All tongues to his true song.
That Pentecostal gust
Now kindles like a tongue
This dark, this simple dust.

Hold back. Do not release
The bell before its time.
Let the long rope of peace
So pregnant in its chime
Through distance gravitate
From pole to silent pole,
Counting with all its weight
The effort of the soul.
Since death and birth obey
One measured harmony,
Shall not the lyre outweigh
The grief-enfolding sea?
When through the bell-rope's span
The music of the just

Has raised the living man,
Give tongue, majestic dust.

Questioning eyes now see
The finite distance move.
How may the company
Of stars preserve his love?
Or who can match the speed
Of whirling nebulae
To the Samaritan's deed
Performed in sympathy?
Not twice, but only once
The evolved in nature stands,
Whether it move in suns
Or pass through living hands.
Now that the starry field
Lies fallen, and the crust
Breaks for the grain to yield,
Give tongue, majestic dust.

THE TOLLING

All is conjecture here
And affirmation there.
Here is the bell man-rung
And there the angel's tongue.
Ah, could the skies reveal
Two spirits in one peal;
But great design has hid
Foreknowledge from the lid.
Here is the reckoning
But there the austere scales swing
Where last is counted first
And confidence reversed.
Yet in the bell we pull
Love's nightingale and bull

Compel a deeper tone
Than either could alone.
Both in the window make
True colours that shall wake
When the last trump is heard;
But Matthew set his word
So firmly that I trace
In dust an angel's face.
The nightingale's dark pain

Heaven's midnight can unchain
Of which this earth's a shade,
And the long love delayed
By that ecstatic tongue
Is always pure and young.
Yet in the bull an old
Earth of momentous mould,
Out of the red marl wrought,
Matches the Maker's thought.
There where a strong shape died
Void air is dignified.
The dying Laocoön,
Tense with his sons in stone,
Wrestling with Fate, blind thralls,
On resurrection calls.
He who, his strength being spent,
Still remained reticent,
Darts his sublime unrest
Into the marvelling breast
Because he did not speak.
Even thus far went the Greek.

Man in his mortal state
Can bear the heavy weight
Of earth and heaven and hell
Compounded in a bell
If he discern the glory

Of John's deep-thundered story
By which a thorn-crowned head
Sinking, to raise the dead,
Has pulled unbounded space
Down, by the weight of grace,
Whose deep-rung moment wins
Forgiveness of all sins.
The impulsive, pagan earth
Gave that proud hunter birth
From whose uplifted hell
The blood of Abel fell.
Yet heaven, since time began,
Loves a reluctant man.
I sigh, for thought has proved
That each, who was so loved,
From stillness can increase
Strength which belongs to peace.

The last, most solemn fires
Teach us that no desires
Can bless as theirs can bless
Who give the wilderness
That dignity of line
From doctrine pounded fine.
In death the fourfold man
Still rules time's bell, and can
Teach the competitive
The loss by which we live.
Deep conflict is the forge
From which their faiths emerge
Who give to humankind
Mind that is more than mind.
The hour when such men die
Translates the galaxy
And keeps, where stars abound,
The selfsame holy ground

Reclaimed from ancient rocks,
Preserved by paradox
Through time and whirling space,
Lost Eden's latter place.

There is no bell that swings,
Though swift as angel's wings,
But answers to the mould
Fiery, primaeval, cold,
In which it first was cast.
Though resurrection's blast
Thrill the resounding nave
And call from niche and grave,
Where sunbeams fall aslant,
Each holy celebrant,
There is no temperate flight
Can raise mankind to light
Save where the font is laid.
Cooled and prepared by shade,
Each must achieve his own
Deliverance from stone,
Pulled by the world to make
True answer, nor to break,
But rise to heaven through weight,
Weaned of an earth made great
Crowning with man-pulled ropes
Those efficacious drops.

I that was born in Wales
Cherish heaven's dust in scales
Which may at dusk be seen
On every village green
Where Tawe, Taff or Wye
Through fields and woods goes by,
Or Western Towy's flame
Write all its watery name
In gold, and blinds our eyes;

For so heaven's joys surprise,
Like music from mild air
Too marvellous to bear
Within the bell's wild span,
The pausing, conscious man.
Who questions at what age
The dead are raised? To assuage
The curious, vision smooths
The lids of age, and youth's.
Even man's defeated hopes
Are variants of these stops
Which, when the god has played,
No creature stands betrayed.

Yet now the bell falls dumb.
Already he is come
Into that other room
So near to his first home.
And I, who set his age
And this last pilgrimage
Against youth's eager quest,
Turned to his point of rest,
Ask what daemonic force
Still holds man to one course.
There is a power from Fate
Which none can estimate,
Held in the godlike reins.
Nothing but dust remains.
How can a stone bell teach
To all men or to each
The ascending fall of those
In whom heaven's scales repose?
Not even the full-starred night
Can put conception right
Till bone be knit with bone.
Then shall their loss be known.

TWO

GEORGE BARKER

The True Confession of George Barker

I

Today, recovering from influenza,
 I begin, having nothing worse to do,
This autobiography that ends a
 Half of my life I'm glad I'm through.
O Love, what a bloody hullaballoo
 I look back at, shaken and sober,
When that intemperate life I view
 From this temperate October.

To nineteen hundred and forty-seven
 I pay the deepest of respects,
For during this year I was given
 Some insight into the other sex.
I was a victim, till forty-six,
 Of the rosy bed with bitches in it;
But now, in spite of all pretexts,
 I never sleep a single minute.

O fellow sailor on the tossing sea,
 O fleeting virgin in the night,
O privates, general in lechery,
 Shun, shun the bedroom like a blight:
Evade, O amorous acolyte,
 That pillow where your heart can bury –
For if the thing was stood upright
 It would become a cemetery.

I start with this apostrophe
 To all apostles of true love:
With your devotion visit me,

Give me the glory of the dove
That dies of dereliction. Give
    True love to me, true love to me,
And in two shakes I will prove
    It's false to you and false to me.

Bright spawner, on your sandbank dwell
    Coldblooded as a plumber's pipe –
The procreatory ocean swell
    Warming, till they're over ripe,
The cockles of your cold heart, will
    Teach us true love can instil
Temperature into any type.

Does not the oyster in its bed
    Open a yearning yoni when
The full moon passes over head
    Feeling for pearls? O nothing, then,
Too low a form of life is, when
    Love, abandoning the cloister,
Can animate the bedded oyster,
    The spawning tiddler, and men.

Thus all of us, the pig and prince,
    The priest and the psychiatrist,
Owe everything to true love, since
    How the devil could we exist
If our parents had never kissed?
    All biographies, therefore,
– No matter what else they evince –
    Open, like prisons, with adore.

Remember, when you love another,
    Who demonstrably is a bitch,
Even Venus had a mother
    Whose love, like a silent aitch,
Incepted your erotic itch.

Love, Love has the longest history,
For we can tell an ape his father
    Begot him on a mystery.

I, born in Essex thirty-four
    Essentially sexual years ago,
Stepped down, looked around, and saw
    I had been cast a little low
In the social register
    For the friends whom I now know.
Is a constable a mister?
    Bob's your uncle, even so.

Better men than I have wondered
    Why one's father could not see
That at one's birth he had blundered.
    His ill-chosen paternity
Embarrasses the fraternity
    Of one's friends who, living Huysmans,
Understandably have wondered
    At fatherhood permitted policemen.

So I, the son of an administer
    Of the facts of civil laws
Delight in uncivil and even sinister
    Violations. Thus my cause
Is simply, friend, to hell with yours.
    In misdemeanours I was nourished –
Learnt, like altruists in Westminster,
By what duplicities one flourished.

At five, but feeling rather young,
    With a blue eye beauty over six,
Hand in hand and tongue to tongue
    I took a sin upon my sex.
Sin? It was pleasure. So I told her.
    And ever since, persisting in

Concupiscences no bolder
  My pleasure's been to undress sin.

What's the point of a confession
  If you have nothing to confess?
I follow the perjuring profession
  – O poet, lying to impress! –
But the beautiful lie in a beautiful dress
  Is the least heinous of my transgressions:
When a new one's added, 'O who was it?'
  Sigh the skeletons in my closet.

Ladybird, ladybird, come home, come home:
  Muse and mistress wherever you are.
The evening is here and in the gloom
  Each bisexual worm burns like a star
And the love of man is crepuscular.
  In the day the world. But, at night, we,
Lonely on egoes dark and far
  Apart as worlds, between sea and sea,

Yearn on each other as the stars hold
  One another in fields together.
O rose of all the world, enfold
  Each weeping worm against the cold
Of the bitter ego's weather:
  To warm our isothermal pride
Cause, sometimes, Love, another
  To keep us by an unselfish side.

The act of human procreation
  – The rutting tongue, the grunt and shudder,
The sweat, the reek of defecation,
  The cradle hanging by the bladder,
The scramble up the hairy ladder,
  And from the thumping bed of Time
Immortality, a white slime,
  Sucking at its mother's udder –

The act of human procreation
   – The sore dug plugging, the lugged out bub,
The small man priming a lactation,
   The grunt, the drooping teat, the rub
Of gum and dug, the slobbing kiss:
   Behold the mater amabilis,
Sow with a saviour, messiah and cow,
   Virgin and piglet, son and sow:

The act of human procreation,
   – O crown and flower, O culmination
Of perfect love throughout creation –
   What can I compare it to?
O eternal butterflies in the belly,
O trembling of the heavenly jelly,
O miracle of birth! Really
   We are excreted, like shit.

2

The Church, mediatrix between heaven
   And human fallibility
Reminds us that the age of seven
   Inaugurates the Reason we
Spend our prolonged seniority
   Transgressing. Of that time I wish
I could recount a better story
Than finding a shilling and a fish.

But memory flirts with seven veils
   Peekabooing the accidental;
And what the devil it all entails
   Only Sigmund Freud suspects.
I think my shilling and my fish
   Symbolised a hidden wish

To sublimate these two affects:
   Money is nice and so is sex.

The Angel of Reason, descending
   On my seven year old head
Inscribed this sentence by my bed:
   The pleasure of money is unending
But sex satisfied is sex dead.
   I tested to see if sex died
But, all my effort notwithstanding,
   Have never found it satisfied.

Abacus of Reason, you have been
   The instrument of my abuse,
The North Star I have never seen,
   The trick for which I have no use:
The Reason, gadget of schoolmasters,
   Pimp of the spirit, the smart alec,
Proud engineer of disasters,
   I see phallic: you, cephalic.

Happy those early days when I
   Attended an elementary school
Where seven hundred infant lives
   Flittered like gadflies on the stool
(We discovered that contraceptives
   Blown up like balloons, could fly);
We memorised the Golden Rule:
   Lie, lie, lie, lie.

For God's sake, Barker. This is enough
   Regurgitated obscenities,
Whimsicalities and such stuff.
   Where's the ineffable mystery,
The affiancing to affinities
   Of the young poet? The history
Of an evolving mind's love
   For the miseries and the humanities?

The sulking and son loving Muse
    Grabbed me when I was nine. She saw
It was a question of self abuse
    Or verses. I tossed off reams before
I cared to recognise their purpose.
    While other urchins were blowing up toads
With pipes of straw stuck in the arse,
    So was I, but I also wrote odes.

There was a priest, a priest, a priest,
    A Reverend of the Oratory
Who taught me history. At least
    He taught me the best part of his story.
Fat Father William, have you ceased
    To lead boys up the narrow path
Through the doors of the Turkish Bath?
    I hope you're warm in Purgatory.

And in the yard of the tenement
    – The Samuel Lewis Trust – I played
While my father, for the rent
    (Ten bob a week and seldom paid),
Trudged London for a job. I went
    Skedaddling up the scanty years,
My learning, like the rent, in arrears,
    But sometimes making the grade.

Oh boring kids! In spite of Freud
    I find my childhood recollections
Much duller now than when I enjoyed
    It. The whistling affections,
All fitting wrong, toy railway sections
Running in circles. Cruel as cats
Even the lower beasts avoid
    These inhumanitarian brats.

Since the Age of Reason's seven
    And most of one's friends over eight,

Therefore they're reasonable? Even
    Sensible Stearns or simpleton Stephen
Wouldn't claim that. I contemplate
    A world which, at crucial instants,
Surrenders to adulterant infants
    The adult onus to think straight.

At the bottom of this murky well
    My childhood, like a climbing root,
Nursed in dirt the simple cell
    That pays itself this sour tribute.
Track any poet to a beginning
    And in a dark room you discover
A little boy intent on sinning
    With an etymological lover.

I peopled my youth with the pulchritude
    Of heterae noun-anatomised;
The literature that I prized
    Was anything to do with the nude
Spirit of creative art
    Who whispered to me: 'Don't be queasy.
Simply write about a tart
    And there she is. The rest's easy.'

And thus, incepted in congenial
    Feebleness of moral power
I became a poet. Venial
    As a human misdemeanour,
Still, it gave me, prisoner
    In my lack of character,
Pig to the Circean Muse's honour.
    Her honour? Why, it's lying on her.

Dowered, invested and endowed
    With every frailty is the poet –
Yielding to wickedness because
    How the hell else can he know it?

The tempted poet must be allowed
    All ethical latitude. His small flaws
Bring home to him, in sweet breaches,
    The moral self indulgence teaches.

Where was I? Running, so to speak,
    To the adolescent seed? I
Found my will power rather weak
    And my appetites rather greedy
About the year of the General Strike,
    So I struck, as it were, myself;
Refused to do anything whatsoever, like
    Exercise books on a shelf.

Do Youth and Innocence prevail
    Over that cloudcuckoo clime
Where the seasons never fail
    And the clocks forget the time?
Where the peaks of the sublime
    Crown every thought; where every vale
Has its phantasy and phantasm
    And every midnight its orgasm?

I mooned into my fourteenth year
    Through a world pronouncing harsh
Judgments I could not quite hear
    About my verse, my young moustache
And my bad habits. In Battersea Park
    I almost heard strangers gossip
About my poems, almost remark
    The bush of knowledge on my lip.

Golden Calf, Golden Calf, where are you now
    Who lowed so mournfully in the dense
Arcana of my adolescence?
    No later anguish of bull or cow
Could ever be compared with half

The misery of the amorous calf
Moonstruck in moonshine. How could I know
    You can't couple Love with any sense?

Poignant as a swallowed knife,
    Abstracted as a mannequin,
Remote as music, touchy as skin,
    Apotheosising life
Into an apocalypse,
    Young Love, taking Grief to wife,
And tasting the bitterness of her lips,
    Forgets it comes from swabbing gin.

The veils descend. The unknown figure
    Is sheeted in the indecencies
Of shame and boils. The nose gets bigger.
    The private parts, haired like a trigger,
Cock at a dream. The infant cries
    Abandoned in its discarded larva,
Out of which steps, with bloodshot eyes,
    The man, the man, crying Ave, Ave!

3

That Frenchman really had the trick
    Of figure skating in this stanza:
But I, thank God, cannot read Gallic
    And so escape his influenza.
Above my head his rhetoric
    Asks emulation. I do not answer.
It is as though I had not heard
    Because I cannot speak a word.

But I invoke him, dirty dog,
    As one barker to another:
Lift over me your clever leg,

Teach me, you snail-swallowing frog
To make out of a spot of bother
    Verses that shall catalogue
Every exaggerated human claim,
    Every exaggerated human aim.

I entreat you, frank villain
    Get up out of your bed of dirt
And guide my hand. You are still an
    Irreprehensible expert
At telling Truth she's telling lies.
    Get up liar; get up, cheat,
Look the bitch square in the eyes
And you'll see what I entreat.

We share, frog, much the same well.
    I sense your larger spectre down
Here among the social swill
    Moving at ease beside my own
And the muckrakers I have known.
    No, not the magnitude I claim
That makes your shade loom like a tall
    Memorial but the type's the same.

You murdered with a knife, but I
Like someone out of Oscar Wilde
    Commemorate with a child
The smiling victims as they die
Slewing in kisses and the lie
    Of generation. But we both killed.
I rob the grave you glorify,
    You glorify where I defiled.

O most adult adulterer
    Preside, now, coldly, over
My writing hand, as to it crowd
    The images of those unreal years

That, like a curtain, seem to stir
   Guiltily over what they cover –
Those unreal years, dreamshot and proud,
   When the vision first appears.

The unveiled vision of all things
   Walking towards us as we stand
And giving us, in either hand,
   The knowledge that the world brings
To those her most beloved, those
   Who, when she strikes with her wings,
Stand rooted, turned into a rose
   By terrestrial understandings.

Come, sulking woman, bare as water,
   Dazzle me now as you dazzled me
When, blinded by your nudity,
   I saw the sex of the intellect,
The idea of the beautiful.
   The beautiful to which I, later,
Gave only mistrust and neglect,
   The idea no dishonour can annul.

Vanquished aviatrix, descend
   Again, long vanished vision whom
I have not known so long, assume
   Your former bright prerogative,
Illuminate, guide and attend
   Me now. O living vision, give
The grave, the verity; and send
   The spell that makes the poem live.

I sent a letter to my love
   In an envelope of stone,
And in between the letters ran
A crying torrent that began
To grow till it was bigger than
Nyanza or the heart of man.

I sent a letter to my love
  In an envelope of stone.

I sent a present to my love
  In a black bordered box,
A clock that beats a time of tears
As the stricken midnight nears
And my love weeps as she hears
The armageddon of the years.
I sent my love the present
  In a black bordered box.

I sent a liar to my love
  With his hands full of roses
But she shook her yellow and curled
Curled and yellow hair and cried
The rose is dead of all the world
Since my only love has lied.
I sent a liar to my love
  With roses in his hands.

I sent a daughter to my love
  In a painted cradle.
She took her up at her left breast
And rocked her to a mothered rest
Singing a song that what is best
Loves and loves and forgets the rest.
I sent a daughter to my love
  In a painted cradle.

I sent a letter to my love
  On a sheet of stone.
She looked down and as she read
She shook her yellow hair and said
Now he sleeps alone instead
Of many a lie in many a bed.

I sent a letter to my love
  On a sheet of stone.

O long-haired virgin by my tree
  Among whose forks hung enraged
A sexual passion not assuaged
  By you, its victim – knee to knee,
Locked sweating in the muscled dark
  Lovers, as new as we were, spill
The child on grass in Richmond Park.

Crying the calf runs wild among
  Hills of the heart are memories:
Long long the white kiss of the young
  Rides the lip and only dies
When the whole man stalks among
  The crosses where remorse lies –
Then, then the vultures on the tongue
  Rule empires of white memories.

Legendary water, where, within
  Gazing, my own face I perceive,
How can my self-disgust believe
  This was my angel at seventeen?
Stars, stars and the world, seen
  Untouched by crystal. Retrieve
The morning star what culprit can
  Who knows his blood spins in between?

Move backward, loving rover, over
  All those unfeathered instances
I tar with kiss of pitch, the dirty
  Lip-service that a jaded thirty
Renders its early innocences.
  Pointer of recollection, show
The deaths in feather that now cover
  The tarry spot I died below.

What sickening snot-engendered bastard
  Likes making an idiot of himself?
I wish to heaven I had mastered
  The art of living like a dastard
While still admiring oneself.
  About my doings, past and recent,
I hear Disgust – my better half –
  'His only decency's indecent.'

Star-fingered shepherdess of Sleep
  Come, pacify regret, remorse;
And let the suffering black sheep
  Weep on the bed it made. Let pause
The orphic criminal to perceive
  That in the venue of his days
All the crimes look back and grieve
  Over lies no grief allays.

Sleep at my side again, my bride,
  As on our marriage bed you turned
Into a flowering bush that burned
  All the proud flesh away. Beside
Me now, you, shade of my departed
  Broken, abandoned bride, lie still,
And I shall hold you close until
  Even our ghosts are broken hearted.

So trusting, innocent, and unknowing
  What the hazards of the world
Storm and strike a marriage with,
  We did not hear the grinders blowing
But sailed our kisses round the world
  Ignorant of monsters and the vaster
Cemetery of innocence. This wreath
  Dreams over our common disaster.

But bright that nuptials to me now
  As when, the smiling foetus carried

Rose-decked today instead of tomorrow,
  Like country cousins we were married
By the pretty bullying embryo
  And you, my friend: I will not borrow
Again the serge suit that I carried
  Through honey of moon to sup of sorrow.

Loving the hand, gentle the reproving;
  Loving the heart, deeper the understanding;
Deeper the understanding, larger the confiding
  For the hurt heart's hiding.
Forgiving the hand, love without an ending
  Walks back on water; giving and taking
Both sides become by simple comprehending:
  Deeper the love, greater the heart at breaking.

4

O Bishop Andrewes, Bishop Berkeley,
  John Peale Bishop and Bishop's Park,
I look through my ego darkly
  But all that I perceive is dark:
Episcopally illuminate
  My parochial testaments
And with your vestal vested vestments
  Tenderly invest my state.

Let grace, like lace, descend upon me
  And dignify my wingless shoulder:
Let Grace, like space, lie heavy on me
  And make me seem a little older,
A little nobler; let Grace sidle
  Into my shameful bed, and, curling
About me in a psychic bridal,
  Prove that even Grace is a darling.

The moon is graceful in the sky,
　　The bird is graceful in the air,
The girl is graceful too, so why
　　The devil should I ever care
Capitulating to despair?
　　Since Grace is clearly everywhere
And I am either here or there
　　I'm pretty sure I've got my share.

Grace whom no man ever held,
　　Whose breast no human hand has pressed,
Grace no lover has undressed
　　Because she's naked as a beast –
Grace will either gild or geld.
　　Sweet Grace abounding into bed
Jumps to it hot as a springald –
　　After a brief prayer is said.

Come to me, Grace, and I will take
　　You close into my wicked hands,
And when you come, make no mistake,
　　I'll disgrace you at both ends.
We'll grace all long throughout the night
　　And as the morning star looks in
And blanches at the state we're in –
　　We'll grace again to be polite.

For Marriage is a state of grace.
　　So many mutual sacrifices
Infallibly induce a peace
　　Past understanding or high prices.
So many forgivenesses for so many
　　Double crossings and double dealings –
I know that the married cannot have any
　　But the most unselfish feelings.

But the wise Church, contemplating
　　The unnatural demands

That marriage and the art of mating
    Make on egoists, commands
We recognise as sacramental
    A union otherwise destined
To break in every anarchic wind
    Broken by the temperamental.

Off the Tarpeian, for high treason,
    Tied in a bag with a snake and a cock,
The traitor trod the Roman rock.
    But in the bag, for a better reason,
The married lovers, cock and snake,
    Lie on a Mount of Venus. Traitor
Each to each, fake kissing fake,
    So punished by a betrayed creator.

'The willing union of two lives.'
    This is, the Lords of Justice tell us,
The purpose of the connubial knot.
    But I can think of only one
Function that at best contrives
    To join the jealous with the jealous,
And what this function joins is not
    Lives, but the erogenous zone.

I see the young bride move among
    The nine-month trophies of her pride,
And though she is not really young
    And only virtually a bride,
She knows her beauties now belong
    With every other treasure of her
Past and future, to her lover:
    But her babies work out wrong.

I see the bridegroom in his splendour
    Rolling like an unbridalled stallion,
Handsome, powerful and tender,
    And passionate as an Italian —

And nothing I could say would lend a
    Shock of more surprise and pride
Than if I said that this rapscallion
    Was necking with his legal bride.

I knew a beautiful courtesan
    Who, after service, would unbosom
Her prettier memories, like blossom,
    At the feet of the weary man:
'I'm such a sensitive protoplasm,'
    She whispered, when I was not there,
'That I experience an orgasm
    If I *touch* a millionaire.'

Lying with, about, upon,
    Everything and everyone,
Every happy little wife
    Miscegenates once in a life,
And every pardonable groom
    Needs, sometimes, a change of womb,
Because, although damnation may be,
    Society needs every baby.

It takes a sacrament to keep
    Any man and woman together:
Birds of a forgivable feather
    Always flock and buck together:
And in our forgivable sleep
    What birdwatcher will know whether
God Almighty sees we keep
    Religiously to one another?

I have often wondered what method
    Governed the heavenly mind when
It made as audience to God
    The sycophant, the seaman sod,
The solipsist – in short, men.
    Even the circus stepping mare

Lifts her nose into the air
   In the presence of this paragon.

For half a dozen simple years
   We lived happily, so to speak,
On twenty-seven shillings a week;
   And, when worried and in tears,
My mercenary wife complained
   That we could not afford our marriage,
'It's twice as much,' I explained,
   'As MacNeice pays for his garage.'

I entertained the Marxian whore –
   I am concerned with economics,
And naturally felt that more
   Thought should be given to our stomachs.
But when I let my fancy dwell
   On anything below the heart,
I found my thoughts, and hands as well,
   Resting upon some private part.

I sat one morning on the can
   That served us for a lavatory
Composing some laudatory
   Verses on the state of man:
My wife called from the kitchen dresser:
   'There's someone here from Japan.
He wants you out there. As Professor.
   Oh, yes. The War just began.'

So Providence engineered her
   Circumstantial enigmas,
And the crown of the objector
   Was snatched from me. In wars
The conscientious protester
   Preserves, as worlds sink to force,
The dignified particular.
   Particularly one, of course.

'The hackneyed rollcall of chronology' –
　　Thus autobiography to de Quincey.
And I can understand it, since he
　　Lived like a footnote to philology.
But the archangelic enumeration
　　Of unpredictable hejiras –
These, with a little exaggeration,
　　I can adduce for my admirers.

And so, when I saw you, nightmare island,
　　Fade into the autumnal night,
I felt the tears rise up for my land,
　　But somehow these tears were not quite
As sick as when my belly laughed
　　Remembering England had given me
The unconditional liberty
　　To do a job for which I starved.

5

Almighty God, by whose ill will
　　I was created with conscience;
By whose merciful malevolence
　　I shall be sustained until
My afflictions fulfil
　　His victories; by whose dispensation
Whatever I have had of sense
　　Has obfuscated my salvation –

Good God, grant that, in reviewing
　　My past life, I may remember
Everything I did worth doing
　　Seemed rather wicked in pursuing:
Grant, Good God, I shall have remitted
　　Those earthly pleasures beyond number

I necessarily omitted,
   Exhausted by the ones committed.

Good God, let me recollect
   Your many mercies, tall and short,
The blousy blondes, the often necked,
   And those whom I should not have thought
Given wisely to me; nor let forget
   My grateful memory the odd
Consolers, too frequently brunette,
   Who charged me for your mercies, God.

Good God, let me so recall
   My grave omissions and commissions
That I may repent them all,
   – The places, faces and positions;
Together with the few additions
   A feeble future may instal.
Good God, only mathematicians
   Consider Love an ordinal.

Good God, so wisely you provided
   The loving heart I suffer with,
That I am constantly divided
   By a deep love for all beneath
Me. Every man knows well
   He rides his own whores down to hell,
But, good God, every knackered horse
   Was, originally, yours.

Good God, receive my thanksgiving
   For all the wonders I have seen
(And all the blunders in between)
   In my thirty odd years of living.
I have seen the morning rise
   And I have seen the evening set –
Anything different would surprise
   Me even more profoundly yet.

Good God, receive my gratitude
    For favours undeserved: accept
This truly heartfelt platitude:
    You gave me too much latitude
And so I hanged myself. I kept
    Your mercy, Good God, in a box
But out at midnight Justice crept
    And axed me with a paradox.

O loving kindness of the knife
    That cuts the proud flesh from the rotten
Ego and cuts the rotten life
    Out of the rotten bone! No, not an
Ounce of sparrow is forgotten
    As that butchering surgeon cuts
And rummages among my guts
    To succour what was misbegotten.

I confess, my God, this lonely
    Derelict of a night, when I
And not the conscious I only
    Feel all the responsibility –
(But the simple and final fact
    That we are better than we act,
For this fortunate windfall
    We are not responsible at all) –

I confess, my God, that in
    The hotbed of the monkey sin
I saw you through a guilt of hair
    Standing lonely as a mourner
Silent in the bedroom corner
    Knowing you need not be there:
I saw the genetic man had torn
    A face away from your despair.

I confess, my God, my Good,
    I have not wholly understood

The nature of our holiness:
    The striking snake errs even less
Not questioning; the physicist
    Not asking why all things exist
Serves better than those who advance a
    Question to which life's the answer.

But, O my God, the human purpose,
    If at all I can perceive
A purpose in the life I live,
    Is to hide in the glass horse
Of our doubt until the pity
    Of heaven opens up a city
Of absolute belief to us,
    Because our silence is hideous

And our doubt more miserable
    Than certainty of the worst would be.
Like infinitely pitiable
    Ghosts who do not even know
They waver between reality
    And unreality, we go
About our lives and cannot see
    Even why we suffer so.

I know only that the heart
    Doubting every real thing else
Does not doubt the voice that tells
    Us that we suffer. The hard part
At the dead centre of the soul
    Is an age of frozen grief
No vernal equinox of relief
    Can mitigate, and no love console.

Then, O my God, by the hand
    This star-wondering grief takes
The world that does not understand
    Its own miseries and mistakes

And leads it home. Not yet, but later
   To lean an expiated head
On the shoulder of a creator
      Who knows where all troubles lead.

6

I looked into my heart to write.
   In that red sepulchre of lies
I saw that all man cherishes
   Goes proud, rots and perishes
Till through that red room pitiless night
   Trails only knife-tongued memories
To whose rags cling, shrieking, bright
   Unborn and aborted glories.

And vinegar the mirages
   That, moaning they were possible
Charge me with the unholy No.
   The unaccomplished issue rages
Round the ringed heart like a bull
   Bellowing for birth. But even so
Remorselessly the clock builds ages
   Over its lifeless embryo.

Ruined empire of dissipated time,
   Perverted aim, abused desire,
The monstrous amoeba cannot aspire
   But sinks down into the cold slime
Of Eden as Ego. It is enough
   To sink back in the primal mud
Of the first person. For what could
   Equal the paradise of Self Love?

The necessary angel is
   The lie. Behind us, all tongue splayed,
The lie triumphant and tremendous
   Shields us from what we are afraid

Of seeing when we turn – the Abyss
    Giving back a face of small
Twisted fear – and this is all,
    To conquer the lie, that we possess.

Come, corybantic self-delusion,
    And whisper such deceptions to
Me now that I will not care who
    Or what you are, save palliation
Of the question marked heart. Let rest
    The harp and horror horned head upon
That green regenerative breast
    By whose great law we still live on.

Now from my window looking down
    I see the lives of those for whom
My love has still a little room
    Go suffering by. I see my own
Stopped, like a stair carpet, at this story
    Not worth the telling. O memory
Let the gilded images of joys known
    Return, and be consolatory!

Bitter and broken as the morning
    Valentine climbs the glaciered sky
With a spike in his foot. The lover's warning
    Blazes a sunrise on our misery:
Look down, look down, and see our grey
    And loveless rendezvous, Valentine:
Fold, then, in grief and cast away
    The love that is not yours or mine.

Of this day of the innocent
    And happy lovers, let me praise
The grotesque bestiary of those
    Who love too much. Monsters invent
Monsters, like babies gypsies raise
    In odd bottles for freak shows –

These love too deeply for the skin.
   Whose bottle are you monster in?

The grotesque bestiary where
   Coiled the pythoness of sighs,
To keep a beast within her there
   Crushes him in her clutch of vice
Till, misshapen to her passion, dead,
   The lion of the heart survives
By suffering kisses into knives
   And a spiked pit into a bed.

Stand in your sad and golden haired
   Accusation about me now,
My sweet seven misled into life.
   Oh had the hot headed seaman spared
Those breast-baring ova on their bough,
   There'd be no aviary of my grief,
No sweet seven standing up in sorrow
   Uttering songs of joy declared

Of joy declared, as birds extol
   The principle of natural pleasure
Not knowing why. Declare to all
   Who disbelieve it, that delight
Naturally inhabits the soul.
   I look down at you to assure
My sense of wrong: but you declare
   Whatever multiplies is right.

I looked into my heart to write.
   But when I saw that cesspit twisted
With the disgusting laws that live
   In royal domination under
The surface of our love, that writhe
   Among our prizes, they attested
The putrefaction of our love
   Spoils the spawner of its grandeur.

7

Today, the twenty-sixth of February,
  I, halfway to the minute through
The only life I want to know,
  Intend to end this rather dreary
Joke of an autobiography.
  Thirty-five years is quite enough
Of one's own company. I grow
  A bit sick of the terrestial stuff.

And the celestial nonsense. Swill
  Guzzle and copulate and guzzle
And copulate and swill until
  You break up like a jigsaw puzzle
Shattered with smiles. The idiotic
  Beatitude of the sow in summer
Conceals a gibbering neurotic
  Sowing hot oats to get warmer.

Look on your handwork, Adam, now
  As I on mine, and do not weep.
The detritus is us. But how
  Could you and I ever hope to keep
That glittering sibyl bright who first
  Confided to us, perfect, once,
The difference between the best and the worst?
  That vision is our innocence.

But we shall step into our grave
  Not utterly divested of
The innocence our nativity
  Embodies a god in. O bear,
Inheritors, all that you have,
  The sense of good, with much care

Through the dirty street of life
　　And the gutter of our indignity.

I sense the trembling in my hand
　　Of that which will not ever lower
Its bright and pineal eye and wing
　　To any irony, nor surrender
The dominion of my understanding
　　To that Apollyonic power
Which, like the midnight whispering
　　Sea, surrounds us with dark splendour.

Enisled and visionary, mad,
　　Alive in the catacomb of the heart,
O lonely diviner, lovely diviner, impart
　　The knowledge of the good and the bad
To us in our need. Emblazon
　　Our instincts upon your illumination
So that the rot's revealed, and the reason
　　Shown crucified upon our desolation.

You, all whom I coldly took
　　And hid my head and horns among,
Shall go caterwauling down with me
　　Like a frenzy of chained doves. For, look!
We wailing ride down eternity
　　Tongue-tied together. We belong
To those with whom we shook the suck
　　And dared an antichrist to be.

Get rags, get rags, all angels, all
　　Laws, all principles, all deities,
Get rags, come down and suffocate
　　The orphan in its flaming cradle,
Snuff the game and the candle, for our state
　　– Insufferable among mysteries –
Makes the worms weep. Abate, abate
　　Your justice. Execute us with mercies!

THOMAS BLACKBURN

A Small, Keen Wind

My wife for six months now in sinister
Tones has muttered incessantly about divorce,
And, since of the woman I'm fond, this dark chatter
Is painful as well as a bit monotonous.
Still, marvel one must, when she fishes out of that trunk,
Like rags, my shadier deeds for all to see
With 'This you did when sober, and that when drunk'
The remarkable powers of memory.
For although I wriggle like mad when she whistles up
Some particularly nasty bit of handy work,
The dirty linen I simply cannot drop,
Since 'Thomas Blackburn' is stitched by the laundry mark.
So I gather the things and say, 'Yes, these are mine,
Though some cleaner items are not upon your list',
Then walk with my bundle of rags to another room
Since I will not play the role of delinquent ghost
And be folded up by guilt in the crook of an arm.
I saw tonight – walking to cool the mind –
A little moonshine on a garden wall
And, as I brooded, felt a small, keen wind
Stroll from the Arctic at its own sweet will.

Teaching Wordsworth

I'm paid to speak, and money glosses
Irrelevance; to keep their places
Students are paid, and so the burden
Is lightened of our mutual boredom
And if the gain's not much, the damage
Is also slight within this college.

'Since for the most part it's subjective
Verse is not anything you might have
In hand or a bank, although it is
Important to some (it is on *our* syllabus)
Concerned with life's outgoing towards death.
Our theme today the poet, Wordsworth

'Who, since not alive still, I disinter
For the sake of a question you will answer,
For the sake also of the vagrant lives
He was involved with, and the wind when it raves
Round such unmarketable places as Scawfell.
An unsociable man and often dull,

'He lived for a long time posthumous
To the "flashing shield", to the great poet he was
Busy for the most part with pedestrian exercise;
However you will not be questioned on those days,
Only the time when with stone footfall
Crags followed him, winds blew through his long skull.

'That, of course, is known as "The Great Period".
Though one hesitates to apply the word "God"
To a poet's theme – it is so manhandled –
Gentlemen, I can offer you nothing instead;
If he himself never applied it to what occurred
When "the light of sense went out", this useful word
Though inaccurate will cut my lecture short,
Being the full stop which ends thought

'And consequently for our purpose useful;
For its brevity you should be grateful.
Anyway for those who "*know*" what the man meant,
My words are – thanks to God – irrelevant.
"Take notes" is the advice I bequeath the rest;
It is a question of self-interest,

'Of being, as Shakespeare says, "to oneself true",
Since the right marks will certainly benefit you.
After all, in the teaching world exam and thesis
For the better posts provide a sound basis,
And in this sense poems are as good as money.
This man's life was a strange journey.

'Early deprived of both father and mother,
To the rocks he returned, to lapping water,
With a sense by deprivation made so acute
That he heard grass speak and the word in a stone's throat;
Many, of course, to silence address their prayer,
But in his case when he spoke it chose to answer,

'And he wrote down, after a certain time-lag,
Their conversation. It is a dialogue
Almost unique in any literature
And a positive gold-mine to the commentator,
For although his words mention what silence said
It can almost any way be interpreted.

'Since to find a yardstick by which the occult
Language of stones can be measured is difficult,
Also that "something far more deeply interfused"
Must be belittled by critiques, if not abused,
There being no instrument with which to measure
This origin of terms and formula

'Which, together with the birth and deathward aim
Of the life in us and things, was this man's theme
As he grew and dwindled into a worse
End of life (as regards verse).
My conclusion is: most words do violence
To what he said. Listen to silence.'

MAURICE CARPENTER

To S.T.C. on his 179th Birthday, October 12th, 1951

There's a brief spring in all of us and when it finishes
The winter must be faced; an uncreative
Dying into darkness, sudden and
Horrible in the line of the face,
Balding, a baggy abdomen, laughable, abominable
Imagine the horror in the mirror! Can there be any
Resurrection after the final realisation
Of down-descent, the reversal of creation?

I have seen snow in April blow across
Hopes; blossoms made Neapolitan, pink cherry
Loaded with cold white crystals, pretty
Confectionery, delicate ambiguity,
As you in Germany suffered a treeless spring,
Snowbound nightingales and a dead child
Coffined in heart's abstraction. You returned
To a ten year chaos, uncreative burning

Of an unfuelled furnace. A belated Beatrice
Nursed the moment they deserted you.
Names. Codes. New handwritings. A new
Start. The letters jumbled up, disguised as Greek,
Fallen abroad, all abroad. The Friend has folded
Its final pages. The crumpled ages speak
Bitterly. I feel about my neck
The Albatross of your inexpiable guilt.

Can there be resurrection after ten years'
Disintegration, newspapers, public life
On a brassy island, walls and no shadows?
The duty and the dispathetic wife
Nag in the mind. Insure your fears
As children die in fantasy. Widowhood

Wanted, the widower wandering.
Talk to locked notebooks wet with tears.

No catalyst, no critical temperature
For the chemical change that flashes in a poem;
A universe of machine components; no
Embodied or embodying whole, living and growing.
The moon that smiled from a sky of opium
No more benign, changed to an inward horror.
Precision of an engine out of action. Given
Such a broken loom, can a new cloth be woven?

Forsaken a moment by the same shaping
Spirit behind the ship, the soul, cold wax,
Congeals on a brass horizon: Imagination
Is walking a narrow gangplank, swaying
Above the milk of the abyss; stations
Of stars, the harbour is at our backs.
The South Pole of our Peace recedes, recedes;
The North Pole of our fear comes nearer, nearer.

Extremes meet. Love is a sudden image,
Agate, unchanging, neither wife nor mother;
A sharp chord in the silence, woman bending over
Children; voices grope for mysteries
Of first speech, minting words and worlds.
The world we know and the world we dream forever
Disparate, a double candle flame.
Can they coincide and be the same?

What more than you can we do? Such love is vulnerable
To the knock of neutrons and the nerve of want.
Friend, on your hundred and seventy ninth
Birthday I turn to you. Could you foresee
The world discarded like a ball of paper?
The hate we face more dangerous, our roots no deeper.
The Lady in the silence bares her dugs
And draws us down to her warm and genial mud.

Needled by no insomnia my sleep is deep.
The nightmare lies in the century's rough kip,
And all the stars upon my childhood ceiling
Fade, flake off; the cradle of the earth
Sways in a void between receding stars.
Neighbour to Venus by a wrinkled Mars,
Our spring delayed, and each demanding birth
Weighs down the walls of our insubstantial dwelling.

Esteecee I have left you while I listed
Our own worries: they were yours as well.
World, word within, the man as child
Delights in future even as eye grows dull.
The bird falls. The weight is at our neck.
The body swings by the idly flapping wheel.
In the roads outside a Jonah century
You paused, and smelled the darkness we know well.

CHARLES CAUSLEY

On Seeing a Poet of the First World War on the Station at Abbeville

Poet, cast your careful eye
Where the beached songs of summer lie,
    White fell the wave that splintered
    The wreck where once you wintered,
White as the snows that lair
Your freezing hair.

Captain, here you took your wine,
The trees at ease in the orchard-line,
    Bonny the errand-boy bird
    Whistles the songs you once heard,
While you traverse the wire,
Autumn will hold her fire.

Through the tall wood the thunder ran
As when the gibbering guns began,
    Swift as a murderer by the stack
    Crawled the canal with fingers black,
Black with your brilliant blood
You lit the mud.

Two grey moths stare from your eyes,
Sharp is your sad face with surprise,
    In the stirring pool I fail
    To see the drowned of Passchendaele,
Where all day drives for me
The spoiling sea.

LAWRENCE DURRELL

On First Looking Into Loeb's Horace

I found your Horace with the writing in it;
Out of time and context came upon
This lover of vines and slave to quietness,
Walking like a figure of smoke here, musing
Among his high and lovely Tuscan pines.

All the small-holder's ambitions; the yield
Of wine-bearing grape, pruning and drainage
Laid out by laws, almost like the austere
Shell of his verses – a pattern of Latin thrift;
Waiting so patiently in a library for
Autumn and the drying of the apples;
The betraying hour-glass and its deathward drift.

Surely the hard blue winterset
Must have conveyed a message to him –
The premonitions that the garden heard
Shrunk in its shirt of hair beneath the stars,
How rude and feeble a tenant was the self,
An Empire, the body with its members dying –
And unwhistling now the vanished Roman bird?

The fruit-trees dropping apples; he counted them;
The soft bounding fruit on leafy terraces,
And turned to the consoling winter rooms
Where, facing south, began the great prayer,
Where his reed laid upon the margins
Of the dead, his stainless authors,
Upright, severe on an uncomfortable chair.

Here, where your clear hand marked up
'The hated cypress' I added 'Because it grew
On tombs, revealed his fear of autumn and the urns',

Depicting a solitary at an upper window
Revising metaphors for the winter sea: 'O
Dark head of storm-tossed curls'; or silently
Watching the North Star which like a fever burns

Away the envy and neglect of the common,
Shining on this terrace, lifting up in recreation
The sad heart of Horace who must have seen it only
As a metaphor for the self and its perfection –
A burning heart quite constant in its station.

Easy to be patient in the summer,
The light running like fishes among the leaves,
Easy in August with its cones of blue
Sky uninvaded from the north; but winter
With its bareness pared his words to points
Like stars, leaving them pure but very few.

He will not know how we discerned him, disregarding
The pose of sufficiency, the landed man,
Found a suffering limb on the great Latin tree
Whose roots live in the barbarian grammar we
Use, yet based in him, his mason's tongue;
Describing clearly a bachelor, sedentary,
With a fond weakness for bronze-age conversation,
Disguising a sense of failure in a hatred for the young,

Who built in the Sabine hills this forgery
Of completeness, an orchard with a view of Rome;
Who studiously developed his sense of death
Till it was all around him, walking at the circus,
At the baths, playing dominoes in a shop –
The escape from self-knowledge with its tragic
Imperatives: *Seek, suffer, endure*. The Roman
In him feared the Law and told him where to stop.

So perfect a disguise for one who had
Exhausted death in art – yet who could guess

You would discern the liar by a line,
The suffering hidden under gentleness
And add upon the flyleaf in your tall
Clear hand: 'Fat, human and unloved,
And held from loving by a sort of wall,
Laid down his books and lovers one by one,
Indifference and success had crowned them all.'

ROY FULLER

What is Terrible

Life at last I know is terrible:
The innocent scene, the innocent walls and light
And hills for me are like the cavities
Of surgery or dreams. The visible might
Vanish, for all it reassures, in white.

This apprehension has come slowly to me,
Like symptoms and bulletins of sickness. I
Must first be moved across two oceans, then
Bored, systematically and sickeningly,
In a place where war is news. And constantly

I must be threatened with what is certainly worse:
Peril and death, but no less boring. And
What else? Besides my fear, my misspent time,
My love, hurt and postponed, there is the hand
Moving the empty glove; the bland

Aspect of nothing disguised as something; that
Part of living incommunicable,
For which we try to find vague adequate
Images, and which, after all,
Is quite surprisingly communicable.

Because in the clear hard light of war the ghosts
Are seen to be suspended by wires, and in
The old house the attic is empty: and the furious
Inner existence of objects and even
Ourselves is largely a myth: and for the sin

To blame our fathers, to attribute vengeance
To the pursuing chorus, and to live
In a good and tenuous world of private values,

Is simply to lie when only the truth can give
Continuation in time to bread and love.

For what is terrible is the obvious
Organization of life: the oiled black gun
And what it cost, the destruction of Europe by
Its councils; the unending justification
Of that which cannot be justified, what is done.

The year, the month, the day, the minute, at war
Is terrible and my participation
And that of all the world is terrible.
My living now must bear the laceration
Of the herd, and always will. What's done

To me is done to many. I can see
No ghosts, but only the fearful actual
Lives of my comrades. If the empty whitish
Horror is ever to be flushed and real,
It must be for them and changed by them all.

DAVID GASCOYNE

An Elegy

R.R. 1916–41

Friend, whose unnatural early death
In this year's cold, chaotic Spring
Is like a clumsy wound that will not heal:
What can I say to you, now that your ears
Are stoppered-up with distant soil?
Perhaps to speak at all is false; more true
Simply to sit at times alone and dumb
And with most pure intensity of thought
And concentrated inmost feeling, reach
Towards your shadow on the years' crumbling wall.

I'll say not any word in praise or blame
Of what you ended with the mere turn of a tap;
Nor to explain, deplore nor yet exploit
The latent pathos of your living years –
Hurried, confused and unfulfilled –
That were the shiftless years of both our youths
Spent in the monstrous mountain-shadow of
Catastrophe that chilled you to the bone:
The certain imminence of which always pursued
You from your heritage of fields and sun . . .

I see your face in hostile sunlight, eyes
Wrinkled against its glare, behind the glass
Of a car's windscreen, while you seek to lose
Yourself in swift devouring of white roads
Unwinding across Europe or America;
Taciturn at the wheel, wrapped in a blaze
Of restlessness that no fresh scene can quench;
In cities of brief sojourn that you pass
Through in your quest for respite, heavy drink
Alone enabling you to bear each hotel night.

Sex, Art and Politics: those poor
Expedients! You tried them each in turn,
With the wry inward smile of one resigned
To join in every complicated game
Adults affect to play. Yet girls you found
So prone to sentiment's corruptions; and the joy
Of sensual satisfaction seemed so brief, and left
Only new need. It proved hard to remain
Convinced of the Word's efficacy; or even quite
Certain of World-Salvation through 'the Party Line' . . .

Cased in the careful armour that you wore
Of wit and nonchalance, through which
Few quizzed the concealed countenance of fear,
You waited daily for the sky to fall;
At moments wholly panic-stricken by
A sense of stifling in your brittle shell;
Seeing the world's damnation week by week
Grow more and more inevitable; till
The conflagration broke out with a roar,
And from those flames you fled through whirling smoke,

To end at last in bankrupt exile in
That sordid city, scene of *Ulysses*; and there,
While War sowed all the lands with violent graves,
You finally succumbed to a black, wild
Incomprehensibility of fate that none could share . . .
Yet even in your obscure death I see
The secret candour of that lonely child
Who, lost in the storm-shaken castle-park,
Astride his crippled mastiff's back was borne
Slowly away into the utmost dark.

The Gravel-Pit Field

Beside the stolid opaque flow
Of a rain-gorged Thames; beneath a thin
Layer of early evening light
Which seems to drift, a ragged veil,
Upon the chilly March air's tide:
Upwards in shallow shapeless tiers
A stretch of scurfy pock-marked waste
Sprawls laggardly its acres till
They touch a raw brick-villa'd rim.

Amidst this nondescript terrain
Haphazardly the gravel-pits'
Rough-hewn rust-coloured hollows yawn,
Their steep declivities away
From the field-surface dropping down
Towards the depths below where rain-
Water in turbid pools stagnates
Like scraps of sky decaying in
The sockets of a dead man's stare.

The shabby coat of coarse grass spread
Unevenly across the ruts
And humps of lumpy soil; loose clumps
Of weeds with withered stalks and black
Tatters of leaf and scorched pods: all
These intertwined minutiae
Of Nature's humblest growths persist
In their endurance here like a rock.

As with untold intensity
On the far edge of Being, where
Life's last faint forms begin to lose
Name and identity and fade
Away into the Void, endures

The final thin triumphant flame
Of all that's most despoiled and bare:
So these last stones, in the extreme
Of their abasement might appear

Like rare stones such as could have formed
A necklet worn by the dead queen
Of a great Pharaoh, in her tomb . . .
So each abandoned snail-shell strewn
Among these botched dock-leaves might seem
In the pure ray shed by the loss
Of all man-measured value, like
Some priceless pearl-enamelled toy
Cushioned on green silk under glass.

And who in solitude like this
Can say the unclean mongrel's bones
Which stick out, splintered, through the loose
Side of a gravel-pit, are not
The precious relics of some saint,
Perhaps miraculous? Or that
The lettering on this Woodbine-
Packet's remains ought not to read:
Mene mene tekel upharsin?

Now a breeze gently breathes across
The wilderness's cryptic face;
The meagre grasses scarcely stir;
But when some stranger gust sweeps past,
Seeming as though an unseen swarm
Of sea-birds had disturbed the air
With their strong wings' wide stroke, a gleam
Of freshness hovers everywhere
About the field: and tall weeds shake,

Leaves wave their tiny flags to show
That the wind blown about the brow
Of this poor plot is nothing less

Than the great constant draught the speed
Of Earth's gyrations makes in Space . . .
As I stand musing, overhead
The zenith's stark light thrusts a ray
Down through dusk's rolling vapours, casts
A last lucidity of day

Across the scene: and in a flash
Of insight I behold the field's
Apotheosis: No-man's-land
Between this world and the beyond,
Remote from men and yet more real
Than any human dwelling-place:
A tabernacle where one stands
As though within the empty space
Round which revolves the Sage's Wheel.

Spring, 1941

Ecce Homo

Whose is this horrifying face,
This putrid flesh, discoloured, flayed,
Fed on by flies, scorched by the sun?
Whose are these hollow red-filmed eyes
And thorn-spiked head and spear-struck side?
Behold the Man: He is Man's Son.

Forget the legend, tear the decent veil
That cowardice or interest devised
To make their mortal enemy a friend,
To hide the bitter truth all His wounds tell,
Lest the great scandal be no more disguised:
He is in agony till the world's end,

And we must never sleep during that time!
He is suspended on the cross-tree now
And we are onlookers at the crime,

Callous contemporaries of the slow
Torture of God. Here is the hill
Made ghastly by His spattered blood

Whereon He hangs and suffers still:
See, the centurions wear riding-boots,
Black shorts and badges and peaked caps,
Greet one another with raised-arm salutes;
They have cold eyes, unsmiling lips;
Yet these His brothers know not what they do.

And on his either side hang dead
A labourer and a factory hand,
Or one is maybe a lynched Jew
And one a Negro or a Red,
Coolie or Ethiopian, Irishman,
Spaniard or German democrat.

Behind His lolling head the sky
Glares like a fiery cataract
Red with the murders of two thousand years
Committed in His name and by
Crusaders, Christian warriors
Defending faith and property.

Amid the plain beneath His transfixed hands,
Exuding darkness as indelible
As guilty stains, fanned by funereal
And lurid airs, besieged by drifting sands
And clefted landslides our about-to-be
Bombed and abandoned cities stand.

He who wept for Jerusalem
Now sees His prophecy extend
Across the greatest cities of the world,
A guilty panic reason cannot stem
Rising to raze them all as He foretold;
And He must watch this drama to the end.

Though often named, He is unknown
To the dark kingdoms at His feet
Where everything disparages His words,
And each man bears the common guilt alone
And goes blindfolded to his fate,
And fear and greed are sovereign lords.

The turning point of history
Must come. Yet the complacent and the proud
And who exploit and kill, may be denied –
Christ of Revolution and of Poetry –
The resurrection and the life
Wrought by your spirit's blood.

Involved in their own sophistry
The black priest and the upright man
Faced by subversive truth shall be struck dumb,
Christ of Revolution and of Poetry,
While the rejected and condemned become
Agents of the divine.

Not from a monstrance silver-wrought
But from the tree of human pain
Redeem our sterile misery,
Christ of Revolution and of Poetry,
That man's long journey through the night
May not have been in vain.

A Vagrant

Mais il n'a point parlé, mais cette année encore
Heure par heure en vain lentement tombera.

Alfred De Vigny

'They're much the same in most ways, these great cities. Of them
  all,
Speaking of those I've seen, this one's still far the best

Big densely built-up area for a man to wander in
Should he have ceased to find shelter, relief,
Or dream in sanatorium bed; should nothing as yet call
Decisively to him to put an end to brain's
Proliferations round the possibilities that eat
Up adolescence, even years up to the late
Thirtieth birthday; should no-one seem to wait
His coming, to pop out at last and bark
Briskly: "A most convenient solution has at last
Been found, after the unavoidable delay due to this spate of wars
That we've been having lately. This is it:
Just fill in (in block letters) on the dotted-line your name
And number. From now on until you die all is
O.K., meaning the clockwork's been adjusted to accommodate
You nicely; all you need's to eat and sleep,
To sleep and eat and eat and laugh and sleep,
And sleep and laugh and wake up every day
Fresh as a raffia daisy!" I already wake each day
Without a bump or too much morning sickness to routine
Which although without order wears the will out just as well
As this job-barker's programme would. His line may in the end
Provide me with a noose with which to hang myself, should I
Discover that the strain of doing nothing is too great
A price to pay for spiritual integrity. The soul
Is said by some to be a bourgeois luxury, which shows
A strange misunderstanding both of soul and bourgeoisie.
The Sermon on the Mount is just as often misconstrued
By Marxists as by wealthy congregations, it would seem.
The "Modern Man in Search of Soul" appears
A comic criminal or an unbalanced bore to those
Whose fear of doing something foolish fools them. *Je m'en fous!*
Blessed are they, it might be said, who are not of this race
Of settled average citizens secure in their *état*
Civil of snowy guiltlessness and showy high ideals
Permitting them achieve an inexpensive lifelong peace
Of mind, through dogged persistence, frequent aspirin, and bile

Occasionally vented via trivial slander . . . Baa,
Baa, O sleepysickness-rotted sheep, in your nice fold
Are none but marketable fleeces. I my lot
Prefer to cast at once away right in
Among the stone-winning lone wolves whose future cells
Shall make home-founding unworthwhile. Unblessed let me go
And join the honest tribe of patient prisoners and ex-
Convicts, and all such victims of the guilt
Society dare not admit its own. I would not strike
The pose of one however who might in a chic ballet
Perform an apache rôle in rags of cleverly-cut silk.
Awkward enough, awake, yet although anxious still just sane,
I stand still in my quasi-dereliction, or but stray
Slowly along the quais towards the ends of afternoons
That lead to evenings empty of engagements, or at night
Lying resigned in cosy-corner crow's-nest, listen long
To sounds of the surrounding city desultorily
Seeking in loud distraction some relief from what its nerves
Are gnawed by: I mean knowledge of its lack of *raison d'être*.
The city's lack and mine are much the same. What, oh what can
A vagrant hope to find to take the place of what was once
Our expectation of the Human City, in which each man might
Morning and evening, every day, lead his own life, and Man's?

The Sacred Hearth
To George Barker

You must have been still sleeping, your wife there
Asleep beside you. All the old oak breathed: while slow,
How slow the intimate Spring night swelled through those depths
Of soundlessness and dew-chill shadow on towards the day.
Yet I, alone awake close by, was summoned suddenly
By distant voice more indistinct though more distinctly clear,
While all inaudible, than any dream's, calling on me to rise
And stumble barefoot down the stairs to seek the air

Outdoors, so sweet and somnolent, not cold, and at that hour
Suspending in its glass undrifting milk-strata of mist,
Stilled by the placid beaming of the adolescent moon.
There, blackly outlined in their moss-green light, they stood,
The trees of the small crabbed and weed-grown orchard,
Perfect as part of one of Calvert's idylls. It was then,
Wondering what calm magnet had thus drawn me from my bed,
I wandered out across the briar-bound garden, spellbound. Most
Mysterious and unrecapturable moment, when I stood
There staring back at the dark white nocturnal house,
And saw gleam through the lattices a light more pure than gold
Made sanguine with crushed roses, from the firelight that all night
Stayed flickering about the sacred hearth. As long as dawn
Hung fire behind the branch-hid sky, the strong
Magic of rustic slumber held unbroken; yet a song
Sprang wordless from inertia in my heart, to see how near
A neighbour strangeness ever stands to home. George, in the wood
Of wandering among wood-hiding trees, where poets' art
Is how to whistle in the dark, where pockets all have holes,
All roofs for refugees have rents, we ought to know
That there can be for us no place quite alien and unknown,
No situation wholly hostile, if somewhere there burn
The faithful fire of vision still awaiting our return.

W. S. GRAHAM

The Ballad of Baldy Bane

Shrill the fife, kettle the drum,
　　My Queens my Sluts my Beauties.
Show me your rich attention
　　Among the shower of empties.
And quiet be as it was once
　　It fell on a night late
The muse has felled me in this bed
　　That in the wall is set.
Lie over to me from the wall or else
　　Get up and clean the grate.

On such a night as this behind
　　McKellar's Tanworks' Wall
It seems I put my hand in hers
　　As we played at the ball.
So began a folly that
　　I hope will linger late,
Though I am of the kitchen bed
　　And of the flannel sheet.
Lie over to me from the wall or else
　　Get up and clean the grate.

Now pay her no attention now,
　　Nor that we keep our bed.
It is yon hoodie on the gate
　　Would speak me to the dead.
And though I am embedded here
　　The creature to forget
I ask you one and all to come.
　　Let us communicate.
Lie over to me from the wall or else
　　Get up and clean the grate.

Make yourself at home here.
   My words you move within.
I made them all by hand for you
   To use as your own.
Yet I'll not have it said that they
   Leave my intention out,
Else I, an old man, I will up
   And at that yella-yite.
Lie over to me from the wall or else
   Get up and clean the grate.

You're free to jig your fiddle or let
   It dally on the bow.
Who's he that bums his chat there,
   Drunk as a wheelbarrow?
Hey, you who visit an old man
   That a young wife has got,
Mind your brain on the beam there
   And watch the lentil pot.
Lie over to me from the wall or else
   Get up and clean the grate.

Now pay her no attention.
   I am the big bowbender.
These words shall lie the way I want
   Or she'll blacklead the fender.
No shallop she, her length and depth
   Is Clyde and clinker built.
When I have that one shafted I
   Allow my best to out.
Lie over to me from the wall or else
   Get up and clean the grate.

Full as a whelk, full as a whelk
   And sad when all is done.
The children cry me Baldy Bane
   And the great catches are gone.

But do you know my mother's tune,
    For it is very sweet?
I split my thumb upon the barb
    The last time I heard it.
Lie over to me from the wall or else
    Get up and clean the grate.

Squeeze the box upon the tune
    They call Kate Dalrymple O.
Cock your ears upon it and
    To cock your legs is simple O.
Full as a whelk, full as a whelk
    And all my hooks to bait.
Is that the nightshift knocking off?
    I hear men in the street.
Lie over to me from the wall or else
    Get up and clean the grate.

Move to me as you birl, Meg.
    Your mother was a great whore.
I have not seen such *pas de bas*
    Since up in Kirriemuir.
I waded in your shallows once,
    Now drink up to that.
It makes the blood go up and down
    And lifts the sneck a bit.
Lie over to me from the wall or else
    Get up and clean the grate.

Through the word and through the word,
    And all is sad and done,
Who are you that these words
    Make this fall upon?
Fair's fair, upon my word,
    And that you shall admit,
Or I will blow your face in glass
    And then I'll shatter it.

Lie over to me from the wall or else
  Get up and clean the grate.

If there's a joke between us
  Let it lie where it fell.
The exact word escapes me
  And that's just as well.
I always have the tune by ear.
  You are an afterthought.
But when the joke and the grief strike
  Your heart beats on the note.
Lie over to me from the wall or else
  Get up and clean the grate.

Full as a whelk, full as a whelk
  My brain is blanketstitched.
It is the drink has floored us
  And Meg lies unlatched.
Lie over to me, my own muse.
  The bed is our estate.
Here's a drink to caulk your seams
  Against the birling spate.
Lie over to me from the wall or else
  Get up and clean the grate.

Now pay her no attention, you.
  Your gears do not engage.
By and large it's meet you should
  Keep to your gelded cage.
My ooze, my merry making muse,
  You're nothing to look at.
But prow is proud and rudder rude
  Is the long and short of that.
Lie over to me from the wall or else
  Get up and clean the grate.

Think of a word and double it.
  Admit my metaphor.
But leave the muscle in the verse,
  It is the Skerry Vor.
Can you wash a sailor's shirt
  And can you wash it white?
O can you wash a sailor's shirt
  The whitest in the fleet?
Lie over to me from the wall or else
  Get up and clean the grate.

Full as a whelk and ending,
  Surprise me to my lot.
The glint of the great catches
  Shall not again be caught.
But the window is catching
  The slow mend of light.
Who crossed these words before me
  Crossed my meaning out.
Lie over to me from the wall or else
  Get up and clean the grate.

Cry me Baldy Bane but cry
  The hoodie off the gate.
Then slowly turn and turn away
  Whatever we have got.
She lies to fell me on the field
  Of silence I wrote.
By whose endeavour do we fare?
  By the word in her throat.
Lie over to me from the wall or else
  Get up and clean the grate.

She lies to fell me on the field
  That is between us here.
I have but to lift the sneck
  With a few words more.

Take kindly to Baldy Bane, then
    And go your ways about.
Tell it in the Causewayside
    And in Cartsburn Street.
Lie over to me from the wall or else
    Get up and clean the grate.

Love me near, love me far.
    Lie over from the wall.
You have had the best of me
    Since we played at the ball.
I cross the Fingal of my stride
    With you at beauty heat,
And I burning words behind me.
    Silence is shouted out.
Lie over to me from the wall or else
    Get up and clean the grate.

JOHN HEATH-STUBBS

To My Brother in Rhodesia

Since blood is thicker than the Mediterranean,
Than the Red Sea, or the Atlantic Ocean,
I frame this message for you out of autumn and darkening,
Wishing it could catch you early in your African spring
(But it is I who in solitude inhabit a dark continent,
Removed into myself to find a further banishment).
The same sun can never shine on us two together,
By the Equator sundered in habitation and weather:
The sun was split for us on the fence of the early garden,
From which we have departed, finding no concord within.
Predestined thus to distance through a common chance of birth,
We have made ourselves into wanderers in the teeth of the earth —
The earth which opens her mouth, not maternal, but an accuser,
And without cease demands the blood of each from the other.
Too quick in love for the rest, I have made you the sole stranger,
Seeking your image in those of whom I may not be keeper.
Displaying thus before me our personal differentiation,
I open not my wound only, but that of a generation,
For everywhere we perceive that natural love is frustrate
Through a failure of clear speaking, and the gift to participate.
We have split suns, and weathers, and worlds. And what shall mend,
Unless this plead forgiveness in the language you don't understand?

Use of Personal Pronouns: A Lesson in English Grammar

I

I is at the centre of the lyric poem,
And only there not arrogant.

'You begin every sentence with *I*' – the rebuke was well taken:
But how on earth else am I to begin them?

YOU AND THOU

You are a secret *thou*.
Fumbling amongst the devalued currency
Of 'dear' and 'darling' and 'my love'
I do not dare to employ it –

Not even in a poem, not even
If I were a Quaker, any more.

Beginning as an honorific, the unaffectionate *you*,
For English speakers, has put *thou* out of business.

So, in our intimate moments,
We are dumb, in a castle of reserve.

And He alone
From Whom no secrets are hid, to Whom
All hearts be open,
Can be a public *Thou*.

HE, SHE AND IT

Only in the third person sex raises its
Unattractive – well, 'head' is a fair enough euphemism.
The thought of sex in which you and I
Do not participate is (unless we are *voyeurs*)
Either horrifying or ridiculous. He and she
He it and she it.

But, moving outside the human order,
We observe there is no personality
Apart from gender. Animals are *it*.
But our own coats, horses and dogs are *he* or *she;*
The huntsman's Puss is *she*, Reynard is *he*;
And even ships are beloved as *she*,
Cars and bicycles, even.

For the homosexual queening it in the Gimcrack Bar
His colleagues, objects of his scandal, are *she*,
While the inaccessible youth in the tight jeans,
Three buttons undone in his scarlet shirt,
Is, however, an *it*.

ONE

One thinks of one as a pronoun employed principally
At Cambridge modestly to include oneself
And other people in one's own set
At Cambridge. One appreciates the French usage
Of *on*; one knows one's Henry James;
One does feel (or, of course, alternatively, one does not)
One must, on the whole, concur with Dr Leavis
(Or, of course, alternatively, with Mr Rylands).
At Oxford, on the other hand,
One tends to become *we*. At Cambridge
One senses a certain arrogance in the Oxford *we*;
A certain exclusiveness in the Cambridge *one*
Is suspected, at Oxford.

WE

'We' said Queen Victoria 'are not amused.'
Subsuming the entire dinner-table into the impersonal
And royal *We*:
No wonder the effect was devastating.

We is also the Editor of *The Times*;
While a Greek chorus is a pattern of dancing *I's*;
The Christian congregation is *I* in the Creed,
Thou in each of the sacraments,
Otherwise solidly *we*. And
'Let Us make man in Our own image.'

We is not amused, nor is it interested
In the possibilities of defeat.

THEY

They is the hellish enemy of paranoiacs
(And even of Auden and Edward Lear);
They is in a conspiracy, is directing hostile thought-waves,
Has got everything fixed *their* way. *They* will not let you.

History a deadly and unending struggle
Of class and national *theys*, except when sometimes
An imperial and oecumenical *We* serenely
Frowns at a barbarian and utter *they*.

But for you and I,
Weeping in our tragic citadel, the horror
Is simply to realise that *they* exist.

PATRICK KAVANAGH

Intimate Parnassus

Men are what they are, and what they do
Is their own business. If they praise
The gods or jeer at them, the gods can not
Be moved, involved or hurt. Serenely
The citizens of Parnassus look on
As Homer tells us, and never laugh
When any mortal has joined the party.
What happens in the small towns –
Hate, love, envy – is not
The concern of the gods. The poet poor,
Or pushed around, or to be hanged, retains
His full reality; and his authority
Is bogus if the sonorous beat is broken
By disturbances in human hearts – his own
Is detached, experimental, subject matter
For ironic analysis, even for pity
As for some stranger's private problem.
It is not cold on the mountain, human women
Fall like ripe fruit while mere men
Are climbing out on dangerous branches
Of banking, insurance and shops; going
To the theatre; becoming
Acquainted with actors; unhappily
Pretending to a knowledge of art.
Poet, you have reason to be sympathetic –
Count them the beautiful unbroken
And then forget them
As things aside from the main purpose
Which is to be
Passive, observing with a steady eye.

Shancoduff

My black hills have never seen the sun rising,
Eternally they look north towards Armagh.
Lot's wife would not be salt if she had been
Incurious as my black hills that are happy
When dawn whitens Glassdrummond chapel.

My hills hoard the bright shillings of March
While the sun searches in every pocket.
They are my alps and I have climbed the Matterhorn
With a sheaf of hay for three perishing calves
In the field under the Big Forth of Rocksavage.

The sleety winds fondle the rushy beards of Shancoduff
While the cattle-drovers sheltering in the Featherna Bush
Look up and say: 'Who owns them hungry hills
That the water-hen and snipe must have forsaken?
A poet? Then by heavens he must be poor'
I hear and is my heart not badly shaken?

On Looking into E. V. Rieu's Homer

Like Achilles you had a goddess for mother,
For only the half-god can see
The immortal in things mortal;
The far-frightened surprise in a crow's flight
Or the moonlight
That stays for ever in a tree.

In stubble fields the ghosts of corn are
The important spirits the imagination heeds.
Nothing dies; there are no empty
Spaces in the cleanest-reaped fields.

It was no human weakness when you flung
Your body prostrate on a cabbage drill –

Heart-broken with Priam for Hector ravaged;
You did not know why you cried,
This was the night he died –
Most wonderful-horrible
October evening among those cabbages.

The intensity that radiated from
The Far Field Rock – you afterwards denied –
Was the half-god seeing his half-brothers
Joking on the fabulous mountain-side.

Epic

I have lived in important places, times
When great events were decided: who owned
That half a rood of rock, a no-man's-land
Surrounded by our pitchfork-armed claims.
I heard the Duffys shouting 'Damn your soul'
And old McCabe stripped to the waist, seen
Step the plot defying blue cast-steel –
'Here is the march along these iron stones'
That was the year of the Munich bother. Which
Was more important? I inclined
To lose my faith in Ballyrush and Gortin
Till Homer's ghost came whispering to my mind
He said: I made the Iliad from such
A local row. Gods make their own importance.

Kerr's Ass

We borrowed the loan of Kerr's big ass
To go to Dundalk with butter,
Brought him home the evening before the market
An exile that night in Mucker.

We heeled up the cart before the door,
We took the harness inside –
The straw-stuffed straddle, the broken breeching
With bits of bull-wire tied;

The winkers that had no choke-band,
The collar and the reins . . .
In Ealing Broadway, London Town
I name their several names

Until a world comes to life –
Morning, the silent bog,
And the god of imagination waking
In a Mucker fog.

The Hero

He was an ordinary man, a man full of humour,
Born for no high sacrifice, to be no marble god;
But all the gods had failed that harvest and someone spread the
    rumour
That he might be deluded into taking on the job.
And they came to him in the spring
And said: you are our poet-king.

Their evil weakness smiled on him and he had no answer to it,
They drove him out of the corners into the public gaze;
And the more he tried to defend himself the more they cried, O poet
Why must you always insult us when we only want to praise?
And he said: I wish you would
Pick on someone else to be your god.

They laughed when he told them he had no intention of dying
For virtue or truth – that his ideal would be
As a mediaeval Sultan, in a middle-class setting enjoying
Many female slaves – where Luxury,

All joyful mysteries,
Takes Wisdom on her knees.

Thinking of the mean reality of middle-class life
They saw the normal as outlandish joy
And all of them embittered with a second-hand wife,
Growing literary, begged him to die
Before his vision became
The slightest bit tame.

He advised them that gods are invisibly cloaked by a crowd,
Mortality touches the conspicuous;
They had the wrong ideas of a god
Who once all known becomes ridiculous.
– I am as obvious as an auctioneer
Dreaming of twenty thousand pounds a year.

At this they roared in the streets and became quite hysterical
And he knew he was the cause of this noise –
Yet he had acted reasonably, had performed no miracle,
Had spoken in a conventional voice,
And he said: surely you can
See that I am an ordinary man?

But instead they rushed off and published in all the papers
And magazines the photograph of their poet genius, god;
And all the cafes buzzed with his outrageous sayings –
And he feared he was beaten and might have to take a job
For one day in the insincere city
He had an attack of self-pity.

He looked in the shoe-shop windows where all the shoes were toys,
Everything else similarly scaled down;
The hotels were doll's houses of doll's vice –
He was trapped in a pygmy town.
Vainly on all fours
He tried the small doors.

Crowds of little men went in with smooth authority
To settle this and that at boardroom tables;
Sometimes they looked up and imagined him Morality,
The silenced bishop of heathen fables,
The ruler of the See
Of monstrous Anarchy.

Yet he found out at last the nature and the cause
Of what was and is he no more wanted
To avoid the ludicrous cheer, the sick applause –
The sword of satire in his hand became blunted,
And for the insincere city
He felt a profound pity.

Lines Written on a Seat on the Grand Canal, Dublin
Erected to the memory of Mrs. Dermot O'Brien

O commemorate me where there is water,
Canal water preferably, so stilly
Greeny at the heart of summer. Brother
Commemorate me thus beautifully.
Where by a lock niagarously roars
The falls for those who sit in the tremendous silence
Of mid-July. No one will speak in prose
Who finds his way to these Parnassian islands.
A swan goes by head low with many apologies,
Fantastic light looks through the eyes of bridges –
And look! a barge comes bringing from Athy
And other far-flung towns mythologies.
O commemorate me with no hero-courageous
Tomb – just a canal-bank seat for the passer-by.

The Hospital

A year ago I fell in love with the functional ward
Of a chest hospital: square cubicles in a row

Plain concrete, wash basins – an art lover's woe,
Not counting how the fellow in the next bed snored.
But nothing whatever is by love debarred,
The common and banal her heat can know.
The corridor led to a stairway and below
Was the inexhaustible adventure of a gravelled yard.

This is what love does to things: the Rialto Bridge,
The main gate that was bent by a heavy lorry,
The seat at the back of a shed that was a suntrap.
Naming these things is the love-act and its pledge;
For we must record love's mystery without claptrap,
Snatch out of time the passionate transitory.

Living in the Country

OPENING

It was the Warm Summer, that landmark
In a child's mind, an infinite day
Sunlight and burnt grass
Green grasshoppers on the railway slopes
The humming of wild bees
The whole summer during the school holidays
Till the blackberries appeared.
Yes, a tremendous time that summer stands
Beyond the grey finities of normal weather.

THE MAIN BODY

It's not nearly as bad as you'd imagine
Living among small farmers in the north of Ireland
They are for the most part the ordinary frightened
Blind brightened, referred to sometimes socially
As the underprivileged.
They cannot perceive Irony or even Satire
They start up with insane faces if

You break the newspaper moral code.
'Language' they screech 'you effing so and so'
And you withdraw into a precarious silence
Organising in your mind quickly, for the situation is tense,
The theological tenets of the press.

There's little you can do about some
Who roar horribly as you enter a bar
Incantations of ugliness, words of half a syllable
Locked in malicious muteness full of glare.
And your dignity thinks of giving up the beer.

But I trained in the slum pubs of Dublin
Among the most offensive class of all –
The artisans – am equal to this problem;
I let it ride and there is nothing over.
I understand through all these years
That my difference in their company is an intrusion
That tears at the sentimental clichés
They can see my heart squirm when their star rendites
The topmost twenty in the lowered lights.
No sir, I did not come unprepared.

Oddly enough I begin to think of Saint Francis
Moving in this milieu (of his own time of course)
How did he work the oracle?
Was he an old fraud, a non-poet
Who is loved for his non-ness
Like any performer.

I protest here and now and forever
On behalf of all my peoples who believe in Verse
That my intention is not satire but humaneness
An eagerness to understand more about sad man
Frightened man, the workers of the world
Without being savaged in the process.
Broadness is my aim, a broad road where the many
Can see life easier generally.

Here I come to a sticky patch
A personal matter that perhaps
Might be left as an unrevealed hinterland
For our own misfortunes are mostly unimportant.
But that wouldn't do.
So with as little embarrassment as possible I tell
How I was done out of a girl,
Not as before by a professional priest but by
The frightened artisan's morality.

It was this way.
She, a shopgirl of nineteen or less
Became infatuated by the old soldier,
The wide travelled the sin-wise.
Desdemona – Othello idea.
O holy spirit of infatuation
God's gift to his poetic nation!

One day her boss caught her glance.
'You're looking in his eyes' he said.
From then on all the powers of the lower orders –
Perhaps all orders – were used to deprive me of my prize
Agamemnon's Briseis.
It soured me a bit as I had
Everything planned, no need to mention what,
Except that it was August evening under whitethorn
And early blackberries.

In many ways it is a good thing to be cast into exile
Among strangers
Who have no inkling
Of The Other Man concealed
Monstrously musing in a field.
For me they say a Rosary
With many a glossary.

F. T. PRINCE

Soldiers Bathing

The sea at evening moves across the sand.
Under a reddening sky I watch the freedom of a band
Of soldiers who belong to me. Stripped bare
For bathing in the sea, they shout and run in the warm air;
Their flesh, worn by the trade of war, revives
And my mind towards the meaning of it strives.

All's pathos now. The body that was gross,
Rank, ravenous, disgusting in the act or in repose,
All fever, filth and sweat, its bestial strength
And bestial decay, by pain and labour grows at length
Fragile and luminous. 'Poor bare forked animal,'
Conscious of his desires and needs and flesh that rise and fall,
Stands in the soft air, tasting after toil
The sweetness of his nakedness: letting the sea-waves coil
Their frothy tongues about his feet, forgets
His hatred of the war, its terrible pressure that begets
A machinery of death and slavery,
Each being a slave and making slaves of others: finds that he
Remembers his old freedom in a game,
Mocking himself, and comically mimics fear and shame.

He plays with death and animality.
And reading in the shadows of his pallid flesh, I see
The idea of Michelangelo's cartoon
Of soldiers bathing, breaking off before they were half done
At some sortie of the enemy, an episode
Of the Pisan wars with Florence. I remember how he showed
Their muscular limbs that clamber from the water,
And heads that turn across the shoulder, eager for slaughter,
Forgetful of their bodies that are bare.
And hot to buckle on and use the weapons lying there.
– And I think too of the theme another found
When, shadowing men's bodies on a sinister red ground,

Another Florentine, Pollaiuolo,
Painted a naked battle: warriors, straddled, hacked the foe,
Dug their bare toes into the ground and slew
The brother-naked man who lay between their feet and drew
His lips back from his teeth in a grimace.

They were Italians who knew war's sorrow and disgrace
And showed the thing suspended, stripped: a theme
Born out of the experience of war's horrible extreme
Beneath a sky where even the air flows
With lacrimae Christi. For that rage, that bitterness, those blows,
That hatred of the slain, what could it be
But indirectly or directly a commentary
On the Crucifixion? And the picture burns
With indignation and pity and despair by turns,
Because it is the obverse of the scene
Where Christ hangs murdered, stripped, upon the Cross. I mean,
That is the explanation of its rage.

And we too have our bitterness and pity that engage
Blood, spirit in this war. But night begins,
Night of the mind: who nowadays is conscious of our sins?
Though every human deed concerns our blood,
And even we must know, what nobody has understood,
That some great love is over all we do,
And that is what has driven us to this fury, for so few
Can suffer all the terror of that love:
The terror of that love has set us spinning in this groove
Greased with our blood.
                              These dry themselves and dress,
Combing their hair, forget the fear and shame of nakedness.
Because to love is frightening we prefer
The freedom of our crimes. Yet, as I drink the dusky air,
I feel a strange delight that fills me full,
Strange gratitude, as if evil itself were beautiful,
And kiss the wound in thought, while in the west
I watch a streak of red that might have issued from Christ's breast.

C. H. SISSON

Money

I was led into captivity by the bitch business
Not in love but in what seemed a physical necessity
And now I cannot even watch the spring
The itch for subsistence having become responsibility.

Money the she-devil comes to us under many veils
Tactful at first, calling herself beauty
Tear away this disguise, she proposes paternal solicitude
Assuming the dishonest face of duty.

Suddenly you are in bed with a screeching tear-sheet
This is money at last without her night-dress
Clutching you against her fallen udders and sharp bones
In an unscrupulous and deserved embrace.

Sparrows Seen from an Office

You should not bicker while the sparrows fall
In chasing pairs from underneath the eaves
And yet you should not let this enraged fool
Win what he will because you fear his grief.

About your table three or four who beg
Bully or trade because those are the passions
Strong enough in them to hide all other lack
Sent to corrupt your heart or try your patience.

If you are gentle, it is because you are weak
If bold, it is the courage of a clown
And your smart enemies and you both seek
Ratiocination without love or reason.

O fell like lust, birds of morality
O sparrows, sparrows, sparrows whom none regards
Where men inhabit, look down now and see
The fury and cupidity of the heart.

Moriturus

The carcase that awaits the undertaker
But will not give up its small voice lies
Hollow and grim upon the bed.

What stirs in it is hardly life but a morosity
Which when this skipped as a child was already under the lids
Rebellious and parting from the flesh.

What drunken fury in adolescence pretended
Merely to possess the flesh and drove onwards
The blind soul to issue in the lap of Venus?

The hope of fatherhood, watching the babe sucking
(Ah, he will grow, hurled headlong into the tomb!)
Gives way to a tenderness spilt into amnesia.

The last chat of corruption reasonable as a syllogism
The image of God is clear, his love wordless
Untie my ligaments, let my bones disperse.

What a Piece of Work is Man

The man of quality is not quite what he was
In the days when that was a technical term
But there are, happily, a number of qualities
You can be a man of, and it is hard if there is not one
In which you can claim distinction.

Like speaks only to like, and without quality
Which you cannot communicate because you have it by blood
Or some subtler misfortune known as intelligence
There can be no speech.
It is by quality that you are not alone.
Those gathered around the bar, as they lift their beer-mugs
Tremble to break the enchantment of what is common:
It is so by the well or the dhobi-ghat
Or the club where charm may not exceed a pattern.
Pray do not address me in Japanese
In which tongue my hopes express themselves ill.
Yet what I have in common with the cat
Suffices for a very short conversation
Each time we meet.

Love is of opposites, they say: but the opposite
Is by way of being a philosophical refinement
And what wedges itself in the female slot
Though apposite enough, is hardly that.
If what goes on there is understanding
Then understanding is something different.
Do not imagine the body cannot lie;
What else have we for lying or for truth?
We talk by species and genus.
God who created us made himself understood
First in the thunder, then in the cloud and then in us.
I wish I did not hear him in the thunder.

How does it happen that the table leg
Has this curve in one age, that in another?
Or that the carved figures of men
Differ more than the men themselves?
Conception rules the art.
How then can one man speak to another?
Is it not the conception
Past any man's thinking, that is expressed

Even in the voice that seems to speak clearly?
And in the million voices that chatter together
Over this peninsula or that continent
A peculiar god looms
And what seems to be said between two people
Is only part of a complex conversation
Which they cannot hear and could not understand.
Yet it is only by taking part in that conversation
That they can give names to their own movements.
I lift my hand: there is a hand, certainly.
I touch your cheek: a hand touches a cheek.
In the name of what god? I have no name of my own.

Can I see my own movement except in conception?
What art has the heart, how does it understand
Its own beat?
The heart opened and the body chilled
Or the mind unneeded because the body is perfect.
The leaves of the jungle are parted. There comes out
One who moves like a deer.
And in the city the tapes record the prices,
Which is also a mode of understanding.

Words are not necessary between bodies.
O admirable attempt to forget to be human.
But you are clothed in words
Less of your own devising than your own body
And of which nothing can strip you but death.
Age and forgetfulness may leave you mumbling,
The words eating your toes or soft belly:
How are you speaking now?

DYLAN THOMAS

The Hunchback in the Park

The hunchback in the park
A solitary mister
Propped between trees and water
From the opening of the garden lock
That lets the trees and water enter
Until the Sunday sombre bell at dark

Eating bread from a newspaper
Drinking water from the chained cup
That the children filled with gravel
In the fountain basin where I sailed my ship
Slept at night in a dog kennel
But nobody chained him up.

Like the park birds he came early
Like the water he sat down
And Mister they called Hey Mister
The truant boys from the town
Running when he had heard them clearly
On out of sound

Past lake and rockery
Laughing when he shook his paper
Hunchbacked in mockery
Through the loud zoo of the willow groves
Dodging the park keeper
With his stick that picked up leaves.

And the old dog sleeper
Alone between nurses and swans
While the boys among willows
Made the tigers jump out of their eyes
To roar on the rockery stones
And the groves were blue with sailors

Made all day until bell time
A woman figure without fault
Straight as a young elm
Straight and tall from his crooked bones
That she might stand in the night
After the locks and chains

All night in the unmade park
After the railings and shrubberies
The birds the grass the trees the lake
And the wild boys innocent as strawberries
Had followed the hunchback
To his kennel in the dark.

Do not go Gentle into that Good Night

Do not go gentle into that good night,
Old age should burn and rave at close of day;
Rage, rage against the dying of the light.

Though wise men at their end know dark is right,
Because their words have forked no lightning they
Do not go gentle into that good night.

Good men, the last wave by, crying how bright
Their frail deeds might have danced in a green bay,
Rage, rage against the dying of the light.

Wild men who caught and sang the sun in flight,
And learn, too late, they grieved it on its way,
Do not go gentle into that good night.

Grave men, near death, who see with blinding sight
Blind eyes could blaze like meteors and be gay,
Rage, rage against the dying of the light.

And you, my father, there on that sad height,
Curse, bless me now with your fierce tears, I pray.
Do not go gentle into that good night.
Rage, rage against the dying of the light.

Vision and Prayer

I

Who
Are you
Who is born
In the next room
So loud to my own
That I can hear the womb
Opening and the dark run
Over the ghost and the dropped son
Behind the wall thin as a wren's bone?
In the birth bloody room unknown
To the burn and turn of time
And the heart print of man
Bows no baptism
But dark alone
Blessing on
The wild
Child.

I
Must lie
Still as stone
By the wren bone
Wall hearing the moan
Of the mother hidden
And the shadowed head of pain
Casting tomorrow like a thorn
And the midwives of miracle sing
Until the turbulent new born
Burns me his name and his flame
And the winged wall is torn
By his torrid crown
And the dark thrown
From his loin
To bright
Light.

When
The wren
Bone writhes down
And the first dawn
Furied by his stream
Swarms on the kingdom come
Of the dazzler of heaven
And the splashed mothering maiden
Who bore him with a bonfire in
His mouth and rocked him like a storm
I shall run lost in sudden
Terror and shining from
The once hooded room
Crying in vain
In the cauldron
Of his
Kiss.

In
The spin
Of the sun
In the spuming
Cyclone of his wing
For I lost was who am
Crying at the man drenched throne
In the first fury of his stream
And the lightnings of adoration
Back to black silence melt and mourn
For I was lost who have come
To dumbfounding haven
And the finding one
And the high noon
Of his wound
Blinds my
Cry.

There
Crouched bare
In the shrine
Of his blazing
Breast I shall waken
To the judge blown bedlam
Of the uncaged sea bottom
The cloud climb of the exhaling tomb
And the bidden dust upsailing
With his flame in every grain.
O spiral of ascension
From the vultured urn
Of the morning
Of man when
The land
And

The
Born   sea
Praised the sun
The   finding   one
And   upright   Adam
Sang   upon   origin!
O the wings of the children!
The woundward flight of the ancient
Young from the canyons of oblivion!
The sky stride of the always slain
In   battle!   the   happening
Of saints to their vision!
The world winding home!
And the whole pain
Flows   open
And   I
Die.

2

In the name of the lost who glory in
The   swinish   plains   of   carrion
Under   the   burial   song
Of the birds of burden
Heavy with the drowned
And the green dust
And   bearing
The ghost
From
The ground
Like   pollen
On the black plume
And the beak of slime
I pray though I belong
Not wholly to that lamenting
Brethren for joy has moved within
The inmost marrow of my heart bone

That he who learns now the sun and moon
Of his mother's milk may return
Before the lips blaze and bloom
To the birth bloody room
Behind the wall's wren
Bone and be dumb
And the womb
That bore
For
All men
The adored
Infant light or
The dazzling prison
Yawn to his upcoming
In the name of the wanton
Lost on the unchristened mountain
In the centre of dark I pray him

That he let the dead lie though they moan
For his briared hands to hoist them
To the shrine of his world's wound
And the blood drop's garden
Endure the stone
Blind host to sleep
In the dark
And deep
Rock
A w a k e
No heart bone
But let it break
On the mountain crown
Unbidden by the sun
And the beating dust be blown
Down to the river rooting plain
Under the night forever falling.

Forever   falling   night   is   a   known
Star   and   country   to   the   legion
Of   sleepers   whose   tongue   I   toll
To   mourn   his   deluging
Light   through   sea   and   soil
And   we   have   come
To   know   all
Places
Ways
Mazes
Passages
Quarters   and   graves
Of   the   endless   fall.
Now   common   lazarus
Of   the   charting   sleepers   prays
Never   to   awake   and   arise
For   the   country   of   death   is   the   heart's   size

And the star of the lost is the shape of the eyes.
In   the   name   of   the   fatherless
In   the   name   of   the   unborn
And   the   undesirers
Of   midwiving   morning's
Hands or instruments
O   in   the   name
Of   no   one
Now or
No
One   to
Be   I   pray
May   the   crimson
Sun   spin   a   grave   grey
And   the   colour   of   clay
Stream   upon   his   martyrdom
In   the   interpreted   evening
And   the   known   dark   of   the   earth   amen.

I turn the corner of prayer and burn
In a blessing of the sudden
Sun. In the name of the damned
I would turn back and run
To the hidden land
But the loud sun
Christens down
The sky.
I
Am found.
O let him
Scald me and drown
Me in his world's wound.
His lightning answers my
Cry. My voice burns in his hand.
Now I am lost in the blinding
One. The sun roars at the prayer's end.

THREE

DANNIE ABSE

Letter to Alex Comfort

Alex, perhaps a colour of which neither of us had dreamt
may appear in the test-tube with God knows what admonition.
Ehrlich certainly was one who broke down the mental doors,
yet only after his six hundred and sixth attempt.

Koch also, painfully and with true German thoroughness
eliminated the impossible, and proved that too many of us
are dying of the same disease. Yet was his green dream,
like yours, fired to burn away an ancient distress.

Still I, myself, don't like Germans, but prefer the unkempt
voyagers, who, like butterflies drunk with suns,
can only totter crookedly in the dazed air
to reach charmingly their destination, as if by accident.

That Greek one then is my hero, who watched the bath water
rise above his navel and rushed out naked, 'I found it,
I found it' into the street in all his shining, and forgot
that others would only stare at his genitals. What laughter!

Or Newton, leaning in Woolsthorpe against the garden wall
forgot his indigestion and all such trivialities,
but gaped up at heaven in just surprise, and with
true gravity, witnessed the vertical apple fall.

O what a marvellous observation! Who would have reckoned
that such a pedestrian miracle could alter history,
that henceforward everyone must fall, whatever
their rank, at thirty-two feet per second, per second?

You, too, I know, have waited for doors to fly open and played
with your cold chemicals and written long letters
to the Press; and listened to the truth afraid and dug deep
into the wriggling earth for a rainbow, with an honest spade.

But nothing rises. Neither spectres, nor oil, nor love.
And the old professor must think you mad, Alex, as you rehearse
poems in the laboratory like vows, and curse those clever scientists
who dissect away the wings and the haggard heart from the dove.

The Game

Follow the crowds to where the turnstiles click.
The terraces fill. Hoompa, blares the brassy band.
Saturday afternoon has come to Ninian Park
and, beyond the goalposts, in the Canton Stand
between black spaces, a hundred matches spark.

Waiting, we recall records, legendary scores:
Fred Keenor, Hardy, in a royal blue shirt.
The very names, sad as the old songs, open doors
before our time when someone else was hurt.
Now, like an injured beast, the great crowd roars.

The coin is spun. Here all is simplified
and we are partisan who cheer the Good,
hiss at passing Evil. Was Lucifer offside?
A wing falls down when cherubs howl for blood.
Demons have agents: the Referee is bribed.

The white ball smacked the crossbar. Satan rose
higher than the others in the smoked brown gloom
to sink on grass in a ballet dancer's pose.
Again, it seems, we hear a familiar tune
Not quite identifiable. A distant whistle blows.

Memory of faded games, the discarded years:
talk of Aston Villa, Orient, and the Swans.
Half-time, the band played the same military airs
as when the Bluebirds once were champions.
Round touchlines the same cripples in their chairs.

Mephistopheles had his joke. The honest team
dribbles ineffectually, no one can be blamed.
Infernal backs tackle, inside forwards scheme,
and if they foul us need we be ashamed?
Heads up! Oh for a Ted Drake, a Dixie Dean.

'Saved' or else, discontents, we are transferred
long decades back, like Faust must pay that fee.
The Night is early. Great phantoms in us stir
as coloured jerseys hover, move diagonally
on the damp turf, and our eidetic visions blur.

God sign our souls! Because the obscure Staff
of Hell rule this world, jugular fans guessed
the result half way through the second half
and those who know the score just seem depressed.
Small boys swarm the field for an autograph.

Silent the Stadium. The crowds have all filed out.
Only the pigeons beneath the roofs remain.
The clean programmes are trampled underfoot
and natural the dark, appropriate the rain,
whilst, under lampposts, threatening newsboys shout.

DRUMMOND ALLISON

Verity

The ruth and truth you taught have come full circle
On that fell island all whose history lies,
Far now from Bramall Lane and far from Scarborough
You recollect how foolish are the wise.

On this great ground more marvellous than Lords
– Time takes more spin than nineteen thirty-four –
You face at last that vast that Bradman-shaming
Batsman whose cuts obey no natural law.

Run up again, as gravely smile as ever,
Veer without fear your left unlucky arm
In His so dark direction, but no length
However lovely can disturb the harm
That is His style, defer the winning drive
Or shake the crowd from their uproarious calm.

Dedication

Had there been peace there never had been riven
Asunder my humility and pride,
My greed and patience. Had I not accepted
The gift of sin I never had been shriven.

Had I not met and missed you in the room,
Had I not lost your body and your leisure,
I had not learned I could dispense with love
Like a blind man unhindered by the gloom.

J. C. ASHBY

Please Don't Laugh

I have given up trying to be grown up
And spend my time in adolescent joys:
Finally thrown my 'I am Jesus' face off
And gone out to the boozer with the boys.

One time I took my stand a little distant
Listened to their jokes and felt superior,
Quivered at the mention of a pair of tits;
Coloured from my toe to my posterior.

For many years I looked round for a model
And two or three times thought I had found one,
But when I tried to pin them down to study,
A boy remained, I found the man had gone.

The first one had a pride that stank like mine did,
The second had a nibble with a tart,
The third one curried favour with the wealthy,
The fourth, poor sod, became obsessed with art.

One more said that he would pin his faith in love
To rid the world of adolescent strife,
But quickly called me outside for a punch-up
When some kind neighbour said I'd jumped his wife.

My mother thought the world was growing rotten,
That God would take His loved ones for His own
Perhaps that's why I sometimes feel so lonely
Playing blues records on the gramophone.

Last week I went out walking in the country
And heard the turtle dove call from a tree,
I didn't stop to listen to his love-song
I knew he wasn't singing it to me.

As I came home I had to pass a cripple
I thought I ought to smile as I went by,
'Now there's someone that you should try and love son,'
I walked straight past, I couldn't meet her eye.

A candidate for office came to our house
'Just look and see sir what my party's done,'
I pointed to a block of flats like barracks
And trees that stood there weeping for the sun.

Kind Dr Best's the one who'll cure my sickness
In his still waiting-room I sit and pray,
He'll give me Soneryl to help the night on
And heart-shaped Drinamyl to cheer the day.

So farewell to the purple-headed mountain,
The family house, the river running by,
Exotic over-ripe fruits in the winter,
The atom bomb that lightens up the sky.

O Father will you cross my brow with water
And place my tired hands upon my chest,
Remove my testicles and their appendage
And teach me how to love with what is left.

WILLIAM BELL

Christmas Elegy
To John Jones

Tonight, the shepherds cry, the sun is risen
for ever; but before their song is done
listen to the murmur of the wind and tide:
tonight for ever sets the unhurried sun,
the flesh for thirty years his prison,
and more – through all the dark and stormy future
        he will not try to hide
    our blemish carven in his side:
tempest and night are blended with his nature.

For darkness is a sermon to remind us
of funerals, and the parade of storms
moves ominously across the midnight sky
to teach that vengeance in a thousand forms
    is ever drawing near behind us.
Yet from our helplessness the sin we fashion
        so very carefully
    is pride, (and none more proud than I
to escape the terrible storms of God's compassion);

Until at a parade or at a sermon
the rows of faces seem remote and strange,
the mind and body are held up by fear
while the accustomed ceremonies change.
    Attired in scarlet and in ermine
deliberately they enter in procession,
        the justices appear
    above the silent court to hear
your accusation and your forced confession.

Enquiry is elaborate execution
prolonged all morning in the market-place
before a curious crowd, who come to stare
as if in infinite time and infinite space
    only those limbs held the solution
of every paradox, now comprehended
        in that admiring square.
    Yet look for no solution there:
that trial has been attempted, and is ended.

O then to your inflexible doom your anguished
mind pursues the prisoners of the past
beneath the storm's displeasure, the midnight's pall,
which will envelop you, unless at last,
    in the last dungeon where they languished
or waited for the rack's exacting science
        perhaps you find a scrawl
    pencilled upon the plaster wall
and marvel at the glorious defiance,

and then you think, whatever degradation
of body, whatever cowardice of the mind
has vexed these prisoners, will be lost to sight
because that challenge makes the judgement blind.
    So after my capitulation
I hope this unsatisfactory letter
        may seem to you to fight
    the tempest and the eternal night
and greet you with the faith of something better.

ANTHONY CRONIN

Lines for a Painter

To Patrick Swift

The tree grew under your hand one day,
So many shades of green growing over the white
Canvas, as though the actual leaves outside the window
And through the open window onto the canvas fell the light.

And I sat on the bed trying unsuccessfully to write,
Envying you the union of the painter's mind and hand,
The contact of brush with canvas, the physical communion,
The external identity of the object and the painting you had planned;

For among the shards of memory nothing that day would grow
Of its own accord,
And I thought I could never see, as you saw the tree on the canvas,
One draughtsman's word.

Only inside the mind,
In the rubble of thought,
Were the pro-and-con, prose-growing, all too argumentative
Poems I sought.

Whereas there in Camden Town
In the petrol fumes and gold of a London summer was the tree you
    drew,
As you might find anywhere, inside or outside the studio, something
Which was itself, not you.

Well envying I have said,
But that evening as we walked
Through the cooling twilight down
To the pub and talked

I saw what in truth I had envied –
Not in fact
That you were released from any obligation,
Or that the act

Of painting was less or more objective
Than thinking the word –
But that, like poems, your painting
Was of course the reward

Of the true self yielding to appearances
Outside its power
While still in the dominion of love asseverating
Its absolute hour.

Elegy for the Nightbound

Tonight in the cold I know most of the living are waiting
For a miracle great as if suddenly ageing money
Repented its rule of the world, all, all of us failing
To find the word which unlocks and would give us something
Better than truth or justice.
And always we find ourselves wanting though all of us enter
The world as a humble supplicant and a lover
And the dream of the child is to grow at last to the stature
His love has attained.
I awoke one night in the mountains
And heard through the falling rain and the breathless darkness
The whispering world say singular third person
We only know what you did we can never know what you wanted,
And not only wicked but foolish, Lord, are the fallen.
And now in the night when the city, gentle with neon,
Calls me from paper where love is an abstract perfection
To the village of friends who are gathered which none ever leaves
I must work out from the fractions of conversation
The total I answer for which is the total I am.

Yet tonight as the twig-breaking winter creeps in through the garden
And the blasphemous Irish are fighting on Hammersmith Broadway
The living pray to the living to recognize difference:
For who can believe that we are but the sum of our actions?
Only the saint and the dead and the deer and the dog.
We are what we want when we love though the wallpaper hates us
And tomorrows founder round a November in fog.
Though nothing remains as you turn to me now at the table
But a circumstance harder to cheat than the words and the white
Page upon which I will put down the poem I'm able
Instead of the one I will never be able to write,
I remember this evening how cold it was there in the evenings,
Lights hung in the trees, the rain goose-flesh on the lake,
And the trees were black, the mountains gone and the rain still
    falling around me
Later when I the singular lay awake.

Responsibilities

My window shook all night in Camden Town
Where through the cutting's murk the sibilant engines
Pounded past slowly gasping in the rain.
Three o'clock was a distant clanking sound.

On Primrose Hill the gasfire in my room
Hissed for more money while the sofa bristled.
The unopened wardrobe stared sepulchrally.
It probably was my predecessor's tomb.

Daily I strolled through leaves to look for letters,
A half of bitter or a chance encounter.
My state was ecstasy, illusion, hunger,
And I was often lectured by my betters.

What wonder that I seldom rose till three
When light was leaking from the grimy primrose

That is the western sky of winter London,
Light in the head, lugubrious, cynical, free.

The past, implausible and profitless,
Is yet a part of us, though I suppose
Gide has the right of it: who have no sense
Of their own history know most happiness.

And yet I set that autumn sunlight down,
That delicate, pale ochre, and that haze;
My eye so idle and the afternoon
So still and timeless with the haze withdrawn.

I could disown them like a thirties poet.
And yet I set inexplicables down;
And scattered images of London when
With a true love I could most truly know it.

The cavernous Rowtons where the footsteps grew
Unsteadily down each corridor and passed
The stages marked on all my bootless journeys,
A pub, a railing and a short way through.

I groped through bomb-sites on the Finchley Road,
Fog in the stomach, blanketed in cold.
Next morning when the gears began to groan
Whatever else I had I had no load.

No more than when in Hammersmith one morning
The sun lit up the Broadway through the fog.
Incarnadine, transported, I was stalking
Besides the early buses in that dawning.

Nightly the wagons splashed along Watling Street,
Battened down, bound for the pool or for the smoke,
Waiting for lifts I did not know myself,
An avatar, a prehistoric beat.

I saw the landscape of old England like
A man upon the moon, amazing shapes,
Wheels, pulleys, engines, slag-heaps, bricks and dirt
And furnace sunsets frowning through the smoke.

And heard the poets of old England too
In Watney's pubs repeating cricket scores
And Dylan stories, talk of our medium
And principles and programmes (radio).

The past, predestined, populous and over
Clings in the dampening leaves, the smell of petrol,
On the brown northern heights where I remember
Highgate and Hampstead in a fine October.

DONALD DAVIE

Barnsley & District

Judy Sugden! Judy, I made you caper
With rage when I said that the British Fascist
Sheet your father sold was a jolly good paper

And you had agreed and I said, Yes, it holds
Vinegar, and everyone laughed and imagined
The feel of the fish and chips warm in its folds.

That was at Hood Green. Under our feet there shone
The modest view, its slagheaps amethyst
In distance and white walls the sunshine flashed on.

If your father's friends had succeeded, or if I
Had canvassed harder for the Peace Pledge Union,
A world of difference might have leapt to the eye

In a scene like this which shows in fact no change.
That must have been the summer of '39.
Yet I go back sometimes, and find nothing strange –

Short circuiting of politics engages
The Grammar School masters still. Their bright sixthformers sport
Nuclear Disarmament badges.

And though at Stainborough no bird's-nesting boy
Nor trespasser from the town in a sunday suit
Nor father twirling a stick can now enjoy

Meeting old Captain Wentworth, in his grey
And ancient tweeds, gun under arm, keen-eyed
And unemployable, and get a gruff Good-day,

His rhododendrons and his laurel hedge
And tussocked acres are not more unkempt
Now that the Hall is a Teachers' Training College.

The parish primary school where a mistress once
Had every little Dissenter stand on the bench
With hands on head, to make him out a dunce;

Blank backs of flourmills, wafer-rusted railings
Where I ran and ran from colliers' boys in jerseys,
Wearing a blouse to show my finer feelings –

These still stand. And Bethel and Zion Baptist,
Sootblack on pavements where the miners' spittle
Starred flattened kerb and greasy flag, persist.

George Arliss was on at the Star, and Janet Gaynor
Billed at the Alhambra, but the warmth
Was no more real then, nor the manners plainer.

And politics has no landscape. The Silesian
Seam crops out in prospects felt as deeply
As any of these, with as much or as little reason.

KEITH DOUGLAS

The Deceased

He was a reprobate I grant
and always liquored till his money went.

His hair depended on a noose from
a Corona Veneris. His eyes, dumb

like prisoners in their cavernous slots, were
settled in attitudes of despair.

You who God bless you never sunk so low
censure and pray for him that he was so;

and with his failings you regret the verses
the fellow made, probably between curses,

probably in the extremes of moral decay,
but he wrote them in a sincere way:

and appears to have felt a refined pain
to which your virtue cannot attain.

Respect him. For this
He had an excellence which you miss.

THOM GUNN

On the Move

'MAN YOU GOTTA GO'

The blue jay scuffling in the bushes follows
Some hidden purpose, and the gust of birds
That spurts across the field, the wheeling swallows,
Have nested in the trees and undergrowth.
Seeking their instinct, or their poise, or both,
One moves with an uncertain violence
Under the dust thrown by a baffled sense
Or the dull thunder of approximate words.

On motorcycles, up the road, they come:
Small, black, as flies hanging in heat, the Boys,
Until the distance throws them forth, their hum
Bulges to thunder held by calf and thigh.
In goggles, donned impersonality,
In gleaming jackets trophied with the dust,
They strap in doubt – by holding it, robust –
And almost hear a meaning in their noise.

Exact conclusion of their hardiness
Has no shape yet, but from known whereabouts
They ride, direction where their tyres press.
They scare, a flight of birds across the field:
Much that is natural, to the will must yield.
Men manufacture both machine and soul,
And use what they imperfectly control
To dare a future on the taken routes.

It is a part isolation, after all.
One is not necessarily discord
On earth; or damned because half animal,
One lacks direct instinct, because one wakes

Afloat on movement that divides and breaks.
One joins the movement in a valueless world,
Choosing it, till, both hurler and the hurled,
One moves as well, always toward, toward.

A minute holds them, who have come to go:
The self-defined, astride the creative will
They burst away; the towns they travel through
Are home for neither bird nor holiness,
For birds and saints complete their purposes.
At worst, one is in motion; and at best,
Reaching no absolute, in which to rest,
One is always nearer by not keeping still.

MICHAEL HAMBURGER

Solidarity

There's honour among thieves, both in and out of prison,
Fellowship even, in the teeth of competition,
And sorority among whores – though mainly off-duty,
On sea-side vacations, or after the ruin of beauty –
But strongest and strangest of all is the solidarity
Of respectable men in respectable company.
Would it be drink that does it? Dissolving differences,
Discrete achievements and individual purities?
No, they feel it when sober, not only at parties and luncheons
But in boardrooms, common rooms, barracks, or charging with
    truncheons.
It comes over them suddenly – not a warm, not a vernal breath,
Yet kindling warmth in cold hearts – the bad conscience of death,
Communist at the frontier bound in time to break through,
But, teacher of love among convicts, Christian too.

BRIAN HIGGINS

The North

Living in the North one gets used to the cold nights
The cities, like stone tongues in the valleys
And the lugged crowds, daft zombies, poured through the streets.

The people are friendly enough, if you'll join them
In the Mecca Meat Market or the boozy clubs.
When you see the men at work as you walk through the cities
You think 'How wild, primitive, dirty and careless'
But when you talk to them in the pubs
You find they like their jobs well enough,
Hand their wives money on a Friday
And respect the intellectual brother-in-law
Who is 'an accountant' or 'head of the costing department'.
Only the pox-bitten old reprobate, drunk in the corner,
Hands us the scraps of profanity we need for our working class novel

They're not a bad lot if you'll join them,
But if you judge them on what they say about queers and the work-
    shy
About sexual offenders generally, or even Teddy Boys shouting,
Then I suppose you would call them a bad lot.
You'd think they were puritanical till you hear their jokes
Or what they did to 'the dirty old pro's' with the army in Naples
And the ones who were in Egypt all know the same bit of Arabic.

At the end of it all you think 'They're just scared of the missus:
Or they like to think they're in the majority
– That's the reason they all defend democracy'

I don't call them a bad lot, but I watch my tongue
– Especially on Saturdays.

The cities are strewn across the North
Like mucky snags that grace a miner's back.

Liverpool, huge and lewd, roaring with black men and knives
And orange angers of race quarrels
Which have never been much more than a chaos of violent bad
    temper,
Race, the formality of an excuse.
If you do it for love or money, and you're under twenty
They call you a Teddy Boy.
Manchester, bigger still, the great pale face of Lancashire.
Spewn in useless fly-blown shops and prosperous slums;
A ganglion of rotting and roaring industrialism
A monstrous rancour of wheels and payment
From glass-blowing St Helens to the grease-filled passageways of
    Oldham

And then the Pennines, waste and mist and lonely sheep
Walls dividing nowhere from nowhere
A tow-headed farmer and the occasional sudden pub.
In the winter you can never see much for the fog and the sleet
In the summer it's like Turkey or somewhere.

Then Huddersfield, Halifax, Bradford and Leeds
With a few banal remarks about the juxtaposition of muck and
    money;
The two great novelists of Bradford, Braine and Priestley
Who sell their novels like so many bales of wool
– Most of them about Batley
Where the rag-merchants marry chorus girls
But not one supposes for breeding purposes
To salt the pedigree and let a bit of red blood into the strain.
There isn't much that's selective in a rag-merchant's ancestry.

Then a gap, while the train or car
Moves through land that is flatter and flatter
– And a lot cleaner into the bargain;
It's almost as if one is coming back into England,
Even the way the talk sounds a bit B.B.C. (rural).

And it's certainly a relief
After travelling across the dustbin lid of limbo
To find oneself back in the dear old world.

The stark rectangle of Hull
With its bombed squares filling up even now
Twenty years after the Luftwaffe gave it a going over
Stands by the wide desolation of the Humber.
A cold clean city full of new pubs
With the worst university in England
Peopled with foreman-lecturers jostling to get reviews in the *Guardian*
Even their names sound like pieces of machinery.

The 'English Department' runs a Critical Quarterly
A kind of correspondence seminar for schoolgirls
That's about as well written as a T.V. advert
A few prim little verses by the interior decorators of the '50s
And critical articles that read like bills of lading.
The library card index is presided over by a sad poet
A beat-up Beverley Nichols all kodaks and missed chances
Out to catch 'the Great Pleasure Loving Public'
What with? a butterfly net?

The new proletarian intellectuals
Who have beer and darts parties ('My father was a crane driver')
All the uniform muddle of the New Left
Competing like hell to get their articles published.
And Lucky-Jimming it up to Senior Lecturer.
Pretending to boast about having a refrigerator
But really winking at knowing what refrigerators stand for.
Interviewing the surrounding chaos and insurance stamping us to
    Elysium
Till the cellars burst and the statistics rattle the ceiling
(I'd rather jump into a tank full of Chablis and to hell with the social
    survey
And social justice into the bargain, if that's what they call it)
DON'T BLAME ME: I'M NOT ADAM.

The flag-wagging milk magnates
Howl beneath the statue of Wilberforce
Encouraging their roundsmen in a piece-work league in three
    divisions
The far-off philanthropists wog-loving their abstract neighbours
With the sacrificial oblation of a tinful of S.A. bananas
And the sacred cry
'Never eat a black man on a Friday.'

O thinking grieves the roots out of the sky
Until we know the blue core of our loss
The crass wind licks our shoulders, the low sun
Plays crucifixion, blood – self parody,
All overdone, the vesperal defeat
Blears in the West and mocks our neat confusion
Time hectors us to graves and dank oblivion
Crawls on our sweating cares:
And thinking piles up lumber in the attic
A load of bricks crashes upon the page
The noise reverberates through dust and files.
No one jumps when sonnets hit the pavement
But 'Watch out' crashes growls a ten-ton diesel
And verbs change levers in the latest jet.

I am the boreal singer. I am North.
I know and hate the factories that made me
The noveau-riche wool magnates with their daughters
Brassbound for Roedean, and their sons
'One's i't business, t'other lad's at Oxford.'
The two-gun culture of the busy rich
Who live in Ilkley and who work in Batley
Dealing in grease, wool bales and foremen.
And leaving t'lass to deal with Dostoevsky.

I know the North that thrums its belts and engines
Brandishing its realism and squalor

Its heavy woollen facts of wealth and power,
Wealth and power my eye,
Tuppeny ha'penny tycoons with weak bladders
And dehydrating lemonading socialism.

I know the North
Its grey faces, closed theatres and stinking shops.
I know the cold wind, the provincial cant.
The football pools sing happy land in Preston
– And it's true that people dress better in London
And the football here is wilder and more local
And when you get up to Scotland the crowds are always fighting
Rangers v. Celtic broken bottles red hair and floods of drunks.

I feel more at home watching Hull Kingston Rovers
And pretending to understand working men
(In one of those clean pubs on the housing estate)
Than sitting on a tatty night club on the Left Bank
With Gregory Corso or somebody
Listening to a lot of political satire
In a language I don't understand.

I have seen the names of Vikings
Scattered through the firmament like dross
The starry dirt that drifts without a compass
In the locked out vacancies beyond the night
Viking names clocked on the woolman's card
And the fierce tribes sounding small down Batley's alley
And the vague clash of old conflicts hollow in the dawn
Where sombre clogs move to the turning day.

The long ship got stuck in Humber mud
The long bones fill with dust by Aire and Calder
The bronze rush died through the feudal years and weary years of
    looms
The Vikings got smaller, the Irish got less swift

The Scotch growled logic and accepted peace
Over the whole North came peace (of a sort) and booze and work
And brass rose like a flower in the desert
And earth which knew the blood of Viking Dane and Celt
Became the property of dreary men.
The blue March wind blows on the Humber
The great rectangular warehouses don beauty
For I know that I will never have to work in them again

And when I forget about builder's labourers
As I walk by the half-grown buildings
Of England's worst university
I will know that I am perfectly safe
As I was at eighteen, the world my early friend.
And once again I will have no theories about Public Assistance.

GEOFFREY HILL

Genesis

1

Against the burly air I strode,
Where the tight ocean heaves its load,
Crying the miracles of God.

And first I brought the sea to bear
Upon the dead weight of the land;
And the waves flourished at my prayer,
The rivers spawned their sand.

And where the streams were salt and full
The tough pig-headed salmon strove,
Curbing the ebb and the tide's pull,
To reach the steady hills above.

2

The second day I stood and saw
The osprey plunge with triggered claw,
Feathering blood along the shore,
To lay the living sinew bare.

And the third day I cried: 'Beware
The soft-voiced owl, the ferret's smile,
The hawk's deliberate stoop in air,
Cold eyes, and bodies hooped in steel,
Forever bent upon the kill.'

3

And I renounced, on the fourth day,
This fierce and unregenerate clay,

Building as a huge myth for man
The watery Leviathan,

And made the glove-winged albatross
Scour the ashes of the sea
Where Capricorn and Zero cross,
A brooding immortality –
Such as the charmed phoenix has
In the unwithering tree.

4

The phoenix burns as cold as frost;
And, like a legendary ghost,
The phantom-bird goes wild and lost,
Upon a pointless ocean tossed.

So, the fifth day, I turned again
To flesh and blood and the blood's pain.

5

On the sixth day, as I rode
In haste about the works of God,
With spurs I plucked the horse's blood.

By blood we live, the hot, the cold,
To ravage and redeem the world:
There is no bloodless myth will hold.

And by Christ's blood are men made free
Though in close shrouds their bodies lie
Under the rough pelt of the sea;

Though Earth has rolled beneath her weight
The bones that cannot bear the light.

Canticle for Good Friday

The cross staggered him. At the cliff-top
Thomas, beneath its burden, stood
While the dulled wood
Spat on the stones each drop
Of deliberate blood.

A clamping, cold-figured day
Thomas (not transfigured) stamped, crouched,
Watched
Smelt vinegar and blood. He,
As yet unsearched, unscratched,

And suffered to remain
At such near distance
(A slight miracle might cleanse
His brain
Of all attachments, claw-roots of sense)

In unaccountable darkness moved away,
The strange flesh untouched, carrion-sustenance
Of staunchest love, choicest defiance,
Creation's issue congealing (and one woman's).

A Pastoral

Mobile, immaculate and austere,
The Pities, their fingers in every wound,
Assess the injured on the obscured frontier;
Cleanse with a kind of artistry the ground
Shared by War. Consultants in new tongues
Prove synonymous our separated wrongs.

We celebrate, fluently and at ease.
Traditional Furies, having thrust, hovered,

Now decently enough sustain Peace.
The unedifying nude dead are soon covered.
Survivors, still given to wandering, find
Their old loves, painted and re-aligned –

Queer, familiar, fostered by superb graft
On treasured foundations, these ideal features!
Men can move with purpose again, or drift,
According to direction. Here are statues
Darkened by laurel; and evergreen names;
Evidently-veiled griefs; impervious tombs.

TED HUGHES

Six Young Men

The celluloid of a photograph holds them well –
Six young men, familiar to their friends.
Four decades that have faded and ochre-tinged
This photograph have not wrinkled the faces or the hands.
Though their cocked hats are not now fashionable,
Their shoes shine. One imparts an intimate smile,
One chews a grass, one lowers his eyes, bashful,
One is ridiculous with cocky pride –
Six months after this picture they all were dead.

All are trimmed for a Sunday jaunt. I know
That bilberried bank, that thick tree, that black wall,
Which are there yet and not changed. From where these sit
You hear the water of seven streams fall
To the roarer in the bottom, and through all
The leafy valley a rumouring of air go.
Pictured here, their expressions listen yet,
And still that valley has not changed its sound
Though their faces are four decades under the ground.

This one was shot in an attack and lay
Calling in the wire, then this one, his best friend,
Went out to bring him in and was shot too;
And this one, the very moment he was warned
From potting at tin-cans in no-man's-land,
Fell back dead with his rifle-sights shot away.
The rest, nobody knows what they came to,
But come to the worst they must have done, and held it
Closer than their hope; all were killed.

Here see a man's photograph,
The locket of a smile, turned overnight

Into the hospital of his mangled last
Agony and hours; see bundled in it
His mightier-than-a-man dead bulk and weight:
And on this one place which keeps him alive
(In his Sunday best) see fall war's worst
Thinkable flash and rending, onto his smile
Forty years rotting into soil.

That man's not more alive whom you confront
And shake by the hand, see hale, hear speak loud,
Than any of these six celluloid smiles are,
Nor prehistoric or fabulous beast more dead;
No thought so vivid as their smoking blood:
To regard this photograph might well dement,
Such contradictory permanent horrors here
Smile from the single exposure and shoulder out
One's own body from its instant and heat.

Hawk Roosting

I sit in the top of the wood, my eyes closed.
In action, no falsifying dream
Between my hooked head and hooked feet:
Or in sleep rehearse perfect kills and eat.

The convenience of the high trees!
The air's buoyancy and the sun's ray
Are of advantage to me;
And the earth's face upward for my inspection.

My feet are locked upon the rough bark.
It took the whole of Creation
To produce my foot, my each feather:
Now I hold Creation in my foot

Or fly up, and revolve it all slowly –
I kill where I please because it is all mine.
There is no sophistry in my body:
My manners are tearing off heads –

The allotment of death.
For the one path of my flight is direct
Through the bones of the living.
No arguments assert my right:

The sun is behind me.
Nothing has changed since I began.
My eye has permitted no change.
I am going to keep things like this.

ELIZABETH JENNINGS

Song at the Beginning of Autumn

Now watch this autumn that arrives
In smells. All looks like summer still;
Colours are quite unchanged, the air
On green and white serenely thrives.
Heavy the trees and growth and full
The fields. Flowers flourish everywhere.

Proust who collected time within
A child's cake would understand
The ambiguity of this –
Summer still raging while a thin
Column of smoke stirs from a land
Proving that autumn gropes for us.

But every season is a kind
Of rich nostalgia. We give names –
Autumn and summer, winter, spring –
As though to unfasten from the mind
Our moods and give them outward forms.
We want the certain, solid thing.

But I am carried back against
My will into a childhood where
Autumn is bonfires, marbles, smoke;
I lean against my window, fenced
From evocations in the air.
When I said autumn, autumn broke.

SIDNEY KEYES

The Island City

Walking among this island
People inhabiting this island city,
Whose coast recedes, whose facile sand
Bears cold cathedrals restively,
I see a black time coming, history
Tending in footnotes our forgotten land.

Hearing the once-virginal
But ageing choirs of intellect
Sing a psalm that would appal
Our certain fathers, I expect
No gentle decadence, no right effect
Of falling, but itself the barren fall:
And Yeats' gold songbird shouting over all.

PHILIP LARKIN

At Grass

The eye can hardly pick them out
From the cold shade they shelter in,
Till wind distresses tail and mane;
Then one crops grass, and moves about
– The other seeming to look on –
And stands anonymous again.

Yet fifteen years ago, perhaps
Two dozen distances sufficed
To fable them: faint afternoons
Of Cups and Stakes and Handicaps,
Whereby their names were artificed
To inlay faded, classic Junes –

Silks at the start: against the sky
Numbers and parasols: outside,
Squadrons of empty cars, and heat,
And littered grass: then the long cry
Hanging unhushed till it subside
To stop-press columns on the street.

Do memories plague their ears like flies?
They shake their heads. Dusk brims the shadows.
Summer by summer all stole away,
The starting-gates, the crowds and cries –
All but the unmolesting meadows.
Almanacked, their names live; they

Have slipped their names, and stand at ease,
Or gallop for what must be joy,
And not a fieldglass sees them home,
Or curious stop-watch prophesies:
Only the groom, and the groom's boy,
With bridles in the evening come.

CHRISTOPHER LOGUE

From Book XXI of Homer's Iliad

PRELUDE

As they retreated towards the river Scamander, Achilles split the
Trojan army: one half, chased back along the same lines the Greeks had
taken yesterday when Hector split their front, ran over the fields towards
Troy; the other half were sealed into a loop made by the Scamander.

Jammed close, these miserable troops slithered down the bank into
deep water, screaming as they twisted away from each other, their
weapons tangled up, hands snatching at chin-straps as the cross cur-
rents sucked them out.

Imagine swarming locusts driven onto a river by fire: the running
flame licks at their armoured skins, singeing them, and, as it huddles
against the water, the swarm is scorched. Likewise Scamander filled
with Trojans.

Into this confusion Achilles waded, hacking amongst the wretched
mass till his arms went numb and the Scamander ran like the gutter set
in the floor of a slaughterhouse. Up to this time the river had not taken
sides; now, soiled by a Greek, Scamander (basing his thoughts on private grievance) began contriving ways to help the Trojans.

Such plans might well have come to nothing. But, while the river
thought, Achilles speared Asteropaeus – grandson of the river Axius –
scooping in the man's belly till his vitals floated out like mauve welts
along Scamander's bank. And after this, Achilles stripped his victim,
stood on his chest and said:

'From a duck's egg, a duck. Doubtless, his relative Scamander
Will cleanse this dead, wet, wreck of an obstinate man.
A River king came in his mother's mother's slit. And proud of it,
He went for me, the one plain King's grandchild, and got killed.
But the axioms commemorating divine peerage, state:
Children from Heaven's one plain King – like me, deadman –
Match above any River's boy exactly as
Above the world's rivers combined at their spring estuaries,
Stands Heaven, stands in Heaven, God.
Consider the Scamander, here. A fine example for any River.

A big River. Surely Scamander would have, if he could have,
Took your part? Ach . . . I hunt a hare with a drum.
Such opposites mock competition, yes, the Freshwater King,
Achelous, plus five wide oceans, plus, O –
Plus the whole damp lot, are good as dead
Faced with God's warning thunder.'
                                   Then Achilles,
Leaving the tall enemy with eels at his white fat
And his tender kidneys infested with nibblers,
Pulled his spear out of the mud and waded off,
After the deadman's troop that beat upstream
For their dead lives; then, glimpsing Achilles' scarlet plume
Amongst the clubbed bullrushes, they ran and as they ran
The Greek got seven of them, swerved, eyeing his eighth, and
Ducked at him as Scamander bunched his sinews up,
And up, and further up, and further further still, until
A glistening stack of water, solid, white with sunlight,
Swayed like a giant bone over the circling humans,
Shuddered, and changed for speaking's sake into humanity.
And the stack of water was his chest; and the foaming
Head of it, his bearded face; and the roar of it –
Like weir-water – Scamander's voice:

'Indeed, Greek, with Heaven helping out, you work
Miraculous atrocities. Still, if God's Son
Has settled every Trojan head on you,
Why make my precincts the scupper for your dead inheritance?
Do them in the fields, Greek, or – or do them anywhere but here.
Thickened with carcasses my waters stiffen in a putrid syrup,
Downstream, the mouth cakes against standing blood-clots yet,
And yet, you massacre. Come, Greek, quit this loathsome rapture!'
                            Head back, Achilles cried:
'Good, River, good . . . and you shall have your way . . . but
    presently.
When every living Trojan squats inside his city's wall.
When I have done with Hector, Hector with me, to death.'

And he bayed and leapt –
Bronze flame shattering like a divine beast –
Pity the Trojans!
And Scamander
Tried involving Lord Apollo:
'Lord, why the negligence?
Is this the way to keep your Father's word?
Time and again he said: Watch the Trojan flank
Till sundown comes, winds drop, shadows mix and lengthen,
War closes down for night, and nobody is out
Bar dogs and sentries.'
Hearing this,
The Greek jumped clear into the water, and Scamander
Went for him in hatred: curved back his undertow, and
Hunched like a snarling yellow bull drove the dead up,
And out, tossed by the water's snout onto the fields;
Yet those who lived he hid behind a gentle wave.
Around the Greek Scamander deepened. Wave clambered
Over wave to get at him, beating aside his studded shield so,
Both footholds gone, half toppled over by the bloodstained crud,
Achilles snatched for balance at an elm, Ah, its roots gave,
Wrenched out, splitting the bank, and tree and all
Crashed square across the river, leaves, splintered branches,
And dead birds blocking the fall. And Achilles wanted out.
Scrambled through the root's lopsided crown, out of the ditch,
Off home.

But the river Scamander had not done with him.
Forcing its bank, an avid lip of water slid
After him, to smother his Greek breath for Trojan victory.
Aoi! – but that Greek could run! – and put and kept
A spearthrow's lead between him and the quick,
Suck, quick, curve of the oncoming water,
Arms outstretched as if to haul himself along the air,
His shield – like the early moon – thudding against
His nape-neck and his arse, fast, fast

As the black winged hawk's full stoop he went –
And what is faster? – yet, Scamander was near on him,
Its hood of seething water poised over his shoulderblades.
Achilles was a quick man, yes, but the Gods are quicker than men.
And easily Scamander's webbed claw stroked his ankles.

You must imagine how a gardener prepares
To let his stored rainwater out, along
The fitted trench to nourish his best plants.
Carefully, with a spade, he lifts the stone
Gagging the throat of his trench, inch by inch,
And, as the water flows, pebbles, dead grubs,
Old bits of root and dusts are gathered and
Swept along by the speed of it, until,
Singing among the plants, the bright water
Overtakes its gardener and his control
Is lost. Likewise Scamander took Achilles.

Each time he stood, looking to see which Part, or whether
Every Part of Heaven's Commonwealth was after him,
The big wave knocked him flat. Up, trying to outleap
The arch of it, Scamander lashed aslant and wrapped his knees
In a wet skirt, scouring the furrows so his toes got no grip.
And Achilles bit his tongue and shrieked, 'Father . . .'
Into the empty sky . . . 'will Heaven help me? No?
Not one of you? Later, who cares? But now? Not now. Not this . . .
Why did my lying mother promise death
Should enter me imaged as Lord Apollo's metal arrowheads?
Or Hector, my best enemy, call Hector for his giant's hit
Over Helen's creditors, and I'll go brave.
Or else my death is waste.
Trapped like a stupid pig-boy beneath dirty water.'

                    In Heaven, two heard him:
First, the woman Prince, Athena; and with her came,
Fishwaisted Poseidon, Lord of the Home Sea.

And dressed as common soldiers they came strolling by,
And held his hand, and comforted him, with:
'Stick, my friend, stick. Swallow the scare for now.
We're with you, and, what's more, God knows it, so
Stick. This visitation means one thing – no River
Will put you down. Scamander? . . . he'll subside . . . and soon.
Now child, do this: Keep after him no matter what.
Keep coming, till
Every living Trojan squats inside his city's wall
And Hector's dead. You'll win. We promise it.'

So the Greek, strong for himself, pushed up, thigh deep,
Towards the higher fields, through water
Bobbing with armoured corpses. Sunlight glittered
Off the intricate visions etched into breastplates
By Trojan silversmiths, and Trojan flesh
Bloomed over the rims of them, leather toggles sunk
To the bone. Picking his knees up, Achilles, now
Punting aside a deadman, now, swimming a stroke or two,
Remembered God's best word and struck
Like a mad-thing at the river. He beat it.
With the palm of his free hand, sliced at it,
At the whorled ligaments of water, yes, sliced at them, Ah! –
There, there-there, and . . . *there* – such hatred,
Scamander had not thought, the woman Prince,
Scamander had not thought, and now, slice, slice,
Scamander could not hold the Greek! Yet,
Would not quit, bent, like a sharp crested hyoid bone,
And sucking Achilles to his midst, called out:
'Simois, let's join to finish off this Greek . . . What's that?
Two against one, you say? Yes. Or Troy is ash,
For our soldiers cannot hold him. Quick, and help, come
Spanned out as a gigantic wave, foot up to peak
A single glinting concave welt, smooth, but fanged
Back in the tumultuous throat of it, with big
Flinty stones, clubbed pumice, trees, and all

Topped by an epaulette of mucid scurf to throttle,
Mash each bone and shred the flesh and drown
The impudence of . . . who apes god.
Listen, Simois . . . nothing can help him now,
Strength, looks, – nothing. Why, that heavy armour, how
It will settle quietly, quietly into ooze,
And his fine white body, aye, slimy and coiled up
I'll suck it down a long stone flue,
And his fellow Greeks will get not one bone back,
And without a barrow to be dug can save their breath
For games.'

        And the water's diamond head
Shut over Achilles, locked round his waist
Film after film of sopping froth, then
Heaved him sideways up while multitudinous crests
Bubbled around his face, blocked his nostrils with the blood
He shed an hour before. And Hera, Heaven's Queen,
Looked over the cloudy battlements of Paradise
And saw it all and saw the Greek was done and cursed Scamander,
Turned to Hephaestus her son, balanced on a silver crutch
And playing with a bag of flames, who, when his mother
Beckoned with her head, came close and listened.
'Little Cripple,' she said, 'would you fight Scamander for me?
Yes?' – rumpling his hair – 'You must be quick, or' –
Giving him a kiss – 'Achilles will be dead. So,
Do it with fire, son; an enormous fire, while' –
Twisting his ear a bit – 'I fetch the white south wind to thrust
Your hot nitre amongst the Trojan dead, and you must
Weld Scamander wet to bank – now! But . . .
Wait. Little One, don't be talked out of it, eh?
More Gods are threatened than struck, Scamander's promises
Are bought. Now, off with you, and, one thing more,
Sear him, Hephaestus, till you hear me shout!'

        And the Fire God
From a carroty fuse no bigger than his thumb,

Raised a burning fan as wide as Troy,
And brushed the plain with it until,
Scamander's glinting width was parched
And the smoke stopped sunlight.

                        Then the garnet coloured bricks
Cooped with whitestone parapets that were Troy's wall,
Loomed in smoky light, like a dark wicket bounding
The fire's destruction.
And Troy's plain was charred and all in cinders
The dead Trojans and their gear. Yet Heaven's Queen
Did not call her son, and the Cripple
Turned on the beaten river.
                    Flames ate at the elms,
Sad willows, clover, tamarisk and galingale
Burst in vermilion flames, heeled through the smoke,
And sank away. Rushes and the green, green lotus bed
Were scorched, and the eels and the pike began to broil.
Last of all, Scamander's back writhed like a burning poultice,
Then, reared up, into a face on fire:

'How can I fight with you, cripple! Flames in my throat,
My waters griddled by hot lacquer! Quit, and I'll quit.
As for Troy and Trojans let 'em burn. Are not we Gods
Above the quarrels of mere humans?'

You must imagine how the water
For boiling down the fat of a juicy pig
After the women pour it in a cauldron,
Seethes and lifts as the kindling takes
And the iron sits in a flamy nest.

Scamander was like this, glazed by the clever Cripple
Who listened only to his Mother. So Scamander called:
'Queen, why does your boy pick on me?
What about other Gods who side with Troy?

I promise to leave off if *he* leaves off. What's more
I swear to turn away when Troy is burnt by Greeks.'

                    So she called the Cripple off.
And between the echoing banks
        Scamander
Rushed gently over his accustomed way.

DOM MORAES

Two Christmas Sonnets

For Pat St John

I. SANTA CLAUS

His sullen kinsmen, by the winter sea,
Said he was holy: then, to his surprise,
They stripped him, flayed him, tied him to a tree
Sliced off his tongue, and burnt out both his eyes.

The trampling reindeer smelt him where he lay,
Blood dyeing his pelt, his beard white with rime,
Until he lurched erect and limped away,
Winter on winter, forward into time.

Then to new houses squat in brick he came
And heard the children's birdlike voices soar
In three soft syllables: they called his name.

The chimney shook: the children in surprise
Stared up as their invited visitor
Lifted his claws above them, holes for eyes.

2. FAMILY DINNER

The spraddled turkey waited for the knife.
The scything holly clashed: the pleading peal
Of bells swung Christ back on a horny heel
To clutch the cross like a desired wife.

And now, pinned there, he flutters till they come,
The gross men and the women they are with,
Who kneel and take his soft flesh in their teeth,
And, chewing the holy cud, flock slowly home.

228

There as the golden children gather by,
Hung with chill bells, the harsh tree is displayed.
A delicate fear wets each child's eye

While the gross father, with the whisky flush
Deepening in his cheeks, prepares the blade
To pare off from the bone the warm white flesh.

MARTIN SEYMOUR-SMITH

Found on a Building Site

'Dear One:
  I am naked on a building site
In Penge West. It is 1.5 a.m., and cold;
The mist wreathes around me, rising in columns.
I shall have much to think of, but chiefly
What shall I do at dawn?
I am writing this with a piece of coal
On a sheet of a tramp's stained newspaper . . .
Dum spiro spero: perhaps you will find this
Before the gaunt sirens of the daybreak speak.
If not, then think of me, but make no enquiries.'

Thus sometimes the poor spirit.

The Administrators

In the administration of culture
Watching our interests, are poetasters
Who wear coloured waistcoats with gold buttons;
Below their suffering countenances,
Like little lights shining upwards,
Sometimes perch bright bow ties.
It is to them we owe those long readings
In public places (we are still allowed to miss them),
Those charming speeches from the stage,
Making us feel at home with the right writers –
A half a glass of *vin ordinaire*,
Rind of high-quality cheese, a stone
(We did not even ask for bread) and a few words with
Themselves: for seven-and-six,
All financed by a government grant.

They had their careers planned at sixteen
Down to the finest detail: even to
Those unhappy verses on lust at twenty-two
(We all knew
And their wives too
That they'd done a thing or two
At twenty-two);
To the later more resonant odes,
Suggesting development though no loss of potency,
On the warmth and blessings of married love –
How they brought a hint of romance perhaps,
A sense of Man's High Predicament
To a rare lady's bed;
To the tauter verses of despair:
The agonized song
That the Bomb is wrong;
To the last, maturing, comfortable,
Swing to the Right.

By the rays of a setting British sun
They sip their old port at thirty-five,
Headily pretending this is Life . . .
Then, sighing, as though hidden cameras
Were recording their creative privacy –
The unconscious beauty of their bearing
Of life's contrastingly so crude burden –
For eager audiences of student-sensitives
Whose applause rings in their well-trained ears,
They retire to beautifully-appointed studies
('Do not disturb me, Penelope')
To pen longish neat stuff on how they yearn, really,
To give it all up, go back to nature, and so on.
(We should say: 'Dear Aunt: I am looking forward
Very much to my holidays this year';
But we do not know enough about
The transformations and transmutations of Art.)

When in the act of composition,
They forget carefully the furtive adultery
In Hampstead High Street, that awful business
On the Heath itself (this is too personal –
The Muse prefers the more dishonest lads);
Put out of mind the slightly embarrassing
Writings of dead men who led different lives,
Though trapped on their shelves and sealed
With fullest explanatory annotations;
Ignore most studiously of all
The letters of refusal they have to write
To those less fortunate but still living
Whose breathing – is it? – somehow stops their pens.

Request on the Field

When I was broken down and unemployed
You found me bitter, wry and under-joyed.
I would not pay my licences or dues,
To vote I did improperly refuse.
So captain-like my shoulder-blade you smote
And cried: 'Up lad! Cast off your sullen coat
And (after you have registered your vote)
Get on the pitch among the knaves and fools
And play the game according to their rules –
They're doing, after all, what you won't do.
Respect them then. Later love comes, too.'

I heeded your wise words, and now am on the field
With shirt and socks and red-cross shield.
But before you dribble off, at captain's call,
Could you explain the absence of a ball?

CHARLES TOMLINSON

On the Hall at Stowey

Walking by map, I chose unwonted ground,
    A crooked, questionable path which led
Beyond the margin, then delivered me
    At a turn. Red marl
Had rutted the aimless track
    That firmly withheld the recompense it hid
Till now, close by its end, the day's discoveries
    Began with the dimming night:

A house. The wall-stones, brown.
    The doubtful light, more of a mist than light
Floating at hedge-height through the sodden fields
    Had yielded, or a final glare
Burst there, rather, to concentrate
    Sharp saffron, as the ebbing year –
Or so it seemed, for the dye deepened – poured
    All of its yellow strength through the way I went:

Over grass, garden-space, over the grange
    That jutted beyond, lengthening-down
The house line, tall as it was,
    By tying it to the earth, tying its pride
(Which submitted) under a nest of barns,
    A walled weight of lesser encumbrances –
Few of which worsened it, and none
    As the iron sheds, sealing my own approach.

All stone. I had passed these last, unwarrantable
    Symbols of – no; let me define, rather
The thing they were not, all that we cannot be,
    By the description, simply of that which merits it:
Stone. Why must (as it does at each turn)

Each day, the mean rob us of patience, distract us
Before even its opposite? – before stone, which
   Cut, piled, mortared, is patience's presence.

The land farmed, the house was neglected: but
   Gashed panes (and there were many) still showed
Into the pride of that presence. I had reached
   Unchallenged, within feet of the door
Ill-painted, but at no distant date – the least
   Our prodigal time could grudge it; paused
To measure the love, to assess its object,
   That trusts for continuance to the mason's hand.

Five centuries – here were (at the least) five –
   In linked love, eager excrescence
Where the door, arched, crowned with acanthus,
   Aimed at a civil elegance, but hit
This sturdier compromise, neither Greek, Gothic
   Nor Strawberry, clumped from the arching-point
And swathing down, like a fist of wheat,
   The unconscious emblem for the house's worth.

Conclusion surrounded it, and the accumulation
   After Lammas growth. Still coming on
Hart's-tongue by maiden-hair
   Thickened beneath the hedges, the corn levelled
And carried, long-since; but the earth
   (Its tint glowed in the house wall)
Out of the reddish dark still thrust up foison
   Through the browning-back of the exhausted year:

Thrust through the unweeded yard, where earth and house
   Debated the terrain. My eye
Caught in those flags a gravestone's fragment
   Set by a careful century. The washed inscription
Still keen, showed only a fragile stem
   A stave, a broken circlet, as

(Unintelligibly clear, craft in the sharp decrepitude)
    A pothook grooved its firm memorial.

Within, wet from the falling roof,
    Walls greened. Each hearth refitted
For a suburban whim, each room
    Denied what it was, diminished thus
To a barbarous mean, had comforted (but for a time)
    Its latest tenant. Angered, I turned to my path
Through the inhuman light, light that a fish might swim
    Stained by the greyness of the smoking fields.

Five centuries. And we? What we had not
    Made ugly, we had laid waste —
Left (I should say) the office to nature
    Whose blind battery, best fitted to perform it
Outdoes us, completes by persistence
    All that our negligence fails in. Saddened,
Yet angered beyond sadness, where the road
    Doubled upon itself I halted, for a moment
Facing the empty house and its laden barns.

ANTHONY THWAITE

The Plausible Bird

Under the winter sun, sitting by the sea,
A bird turned on a wing and said to me:
'Why do you thus sit idly by the shore
Making your head and arse so red and sore?'

'I make a poem, bird, inside my head
And watch the winter waves come on,' I said.
'Show me the words you make, and what you see
Across the waves,' the bird demanded me.

'Grey,' I said idly, 'and the sun, the sky,
Various vestiges of the sea. And I
Comprehend also you, small bird, as one
Of the bright minor creatures under the sun,

Possible meat for poems I may write.'
'What makes the sea, or closes up the light?'
Enquired the irrelevant bird. 'Foolish,' I said
'Do you not hear the rhythms in my head

Engendering images, or clever rhymes
Erupting?' 'You compose in seismic times,'
Said the weak, scatterbrained and facile bird;
'Last week I sat upon a branch and heard

Various rumours creasing the vague air,
Lies, propaganda, guns. I should beware
Of sitting in bleak headlands writing verse,
For fire and smoke seem to be growing worse

Across the bay. Describe the sea,' he said.
'Immense, cold,' I began . . . 'And vast, and sad –

I know,' he chirped, 'I've heard it all. Now me –
Describe me, and say only what you see.'

'A small and beadlike bird, clockwork and smart,
Acknowledging little of what constitutes art,'
Pompous, I answered him. 'Poor boy,' he sang,
'I weep to see your tatty world go bang.

Watch me,' he said, 'for I am Living Art
(In capitals). I am the Human Heart.
Farewell.' And as he flew away, bright one,
He interposed a dropping in the sun.